just eat

ALSO BY JESSIE JAMES DECKER

Just Jessie:
My Guide to Love, Life, Family, and Food

Just Feed Me:
Simply Delicious Recipes from My Heart to Your Plate

just eat

More Than 100 Easy
and Delicious Recipes
That Taste Just Like Home

Jessie James Decker

DEYST.

An Imprint of WILLIAM MORROW

I want to dedicate this book to my family.

To my love, Eric, and my beautiful babies.
Y'all make my heart full. I love you.

And, of course, to my amazing fans.
I get to make another cookbook,
and it's all because of you! Thank you
for your ongoing love and support.

Contents

Introduction

Y'all know I'm a foodie—always have been—and my love of delicious food only continues to grow stronger over the years. The more I learn about food, new ways to use ingredients, and the way other cultures cook, the more I want to try new recipes and add my own twist. My first book, *Just Feed Me*, is a tried-and-true cookbook of comfort foods and recipes I've been cooking in the kitchen for my family for years. When my publisher asked me what I wanted my second cookbook to be about, I thought on it for a couple of months and the answer became so clear: *Just Eat*—a follow-up to my first cookbook, but with even more. I don't have just one style of cooking.

For those who don't have my other books, I was born in Italy and lived in fourteen different places growing up. My roots are tied to so many places, which has really influenced how I cook. I would have a tough time just choosing one style to fill up a book. My whole family is from Louisiana, so Cajun food was the core of my childhood meals, but we also have Italian and Greek roots that come through in what we cook. Growing up all over the United States, I picked up cooking styles from everywhere—Texas and Georgia, coastal cooking in the Gulf, my husband Eric's Minnesota influences, and so many more places. *Just Eat* is as comforting and delicious as *Just Feed Me*, but with even more family recipes plus new recipes I've learned and fallen in love with over the past two years.

Since my last cookbook, Eric built the most beautiful garden for us to grow our own herbs, fruits, and vegetables, and this has added so much to the way I cook now. I also ask more questions when I go to restaurants and speak to other home cooks and chefs, so I can learn more for myself as a home chef.

> *I learned that less is more and that it's key to use true and real ingredients.*

Just Eat has more easy on-the-go recipes, coastal, Cajun, and family-style dishes, healthy foods to eat while trying to get fit—and even a simple immunity-boost recipe to recharge and reboot your body after a food-and-drink-filled vacation.

Speaking of vacation, in May and June 2021 my family and I took a twenty-six-day trip to Greece and Italy, island- and city-hopping. I got to cook alongside some of the most incredible cooks and learn so much more about food in many ways I had never thought of. What do they do differently than we do? I learned that less is more and that it's key to use true and real ingredients. What blew my mind is how flavorful the food was with way fewer ingredients and so little seasoning. I decided to take a lot of these food philosophies and bring them back home. Something else I loved? These cooks all keep a garden. Having a mini garden is more common than having a washing machine. I would stand overlooking a city in Italy or Greece with a glass of delicious wine as the sun set. I'd look out across the little towns at all the flats with clothes hanging out on a line, and I'd imagine what the lives of the people who lived inside were like. I could see into the courtyards, see their mini herb gardens and lemon trees, and I was fascinated. It's a priority there to have fresh herbs, and it takes so little to build a garden to plant them. They take these minimal ingredients and can create the most delicious meals too. I learned to use just the ingredients in my garden to cook the freshest meals. I'm so excited to share a chapter solely dedicated to my food adventures in Greece and Italy, with lots of family photos from an unforgettable experience.

Just Eat is more comfort, more love, and more recipes from my heart to your kitchen table. I know y'all are going to love this book just as much, and I can't wait to see your favorites that you whip up this time.

Before We Start Heating Things Up!

I don't follow a lot of typical cooking rules in my kitchen because I go by flavor and the way I've learned to cook through years of watching my mama and cooking for my family. But there are three things I can't live without when I'm cooking: salt, pepper, and garlic powder.

Seasoning can make or break a meal for me, so even when I'm on vacation or traveling, I make sure I have those three seasonings handy. I love sea salt because it's a little less processed than your average table salt, and it has some minerals in it too.

Then there's freshly ground black pepper, which, if you can keep it on hand, is always better to give that punch of peppery flavor. I like to keep a little pepper grinder on hand, so I can grind it fresh as I need it!

Garlic powder doesn't need an explanation because garlic makes almost everything savory taste better. Even when I'm cooking with fresh garlic, I add a hint of concentrated powder to bring out the flavor even more.

Always have those on hand along with a good wooden spoon, and you're good to go!

"Good for Ya!" Sticker

The recipes stamped with the "Good for Ya!" sticker are not your typical fad diet foods. These are the foods I use to fuel my body; they boost my energy while satisfying my appetite. All of them are veggie-forward, full of protein, or high in fiber—and they all taste amazing.

I eat what I want, but I also need to work out and be active so I can do that. I focus on the foods I love in the right portion sizes for me. I am stronger and have more energy than ever. My life is less about counting calories and more about eating real food. This shift has helped me so much, and I love my body more than ever.

1

Breakfast foods are my favorite. They're hearty and comforting, and they start my day off right. And brunch is . . . even better. It's the perfect combo of savory and sweet with an anything-goes policy. There are times when I don't want to eat breakfast until 2:00 in the afternoon—it's still perfectly acceptable to eat waffles and a mimosa with a side of fries.

Good Morning, Darlin' Breakfast + Brunch

Recipes with ○ icon indicate "Good for Ya!" recipes.

Lemon-Ginger Immunity Shots

MAKES 2 TO 3 SERVINGS

PREP TIME: 10 minutes

I try and do one of these shots daily! You have to be tough, because it will burn going down, but the benefits are so worth it.

½ cup fresh lemon juice (from about 4 lemons)

One 1- to 2-inch piece peeled fresh ginger

½ teaspoon oregano oil

Pinch of cayenne pepper

Pinch of ground turmeric

Pinch of ground ginger

1. Add the lemon juice and ginger to a blender or food processor and blend until no longer chunky; this could take 3 to 5 minutes or more depending on your machine.

2. Strain the mixture through a fine-mesh strainer into a large measuring cup. Pour in the oil, then divide the liquid between two or three shot glasses.

3. Dust each glass rim with cayenne, turmeric, and ground ginger and shoot it.

Benefits of my immunity shots:

+ Boost immunity
+ Improve your mood instantly
+ Calm stomachaches
+ Reduce menstrual cramps and bloating
+ Fight colds and infections

+ Energize your workout
+ Support weight loss by triggering metabolism
+ Regulate blood sugar
+ Help lower blood pressure

Get Fit Strawberry Smoothies

**MAKES
2 SERVINGS**

PREP TIME:
5 minutes

In our house smoothies are a big thing. They're a great way to get in a nice protein boost after a workout or to get your day going when you're in a hurry and need something quick and nourishing. This one in particular is my daughter Vivi's favorite on gymnastics days when she's working hard and needs that fuel for practice, because it's sweet and creamy and tastes like a strawberry milkshake.

1½ cups unsweetened vanilla almond milk, plus more if needed

1 frozen banana, sliced into medallions

2 cups strawberries

½ cup vanilla Greek yogurt, plus more if needed

2 tablespoons vanilla protein powder

Strawverry slices, for garnish

1. Place all the ingredients in a high-speed blender and blend until smooth and creamy, about 1 minute.

2. Taste and adjust with a little more milk or yogurt to get your desired consistency. Pour into two glasses, garnish with strawberry slices, and enjoy!

Cozy Overnight Oats

**MAKES
2 SERVINGS**

PREP TIME:
5 minutes

CHILL TIME:
4 to 8 hours

Some mornings I am too busy for anything that isn't grab-and-go, which is why I love having these yummy overnight oats stocked and ready in the fridge. They are so simple and can be tailored to whatever flavors you like and the health goals you're working on. This one recipe can make so many different variations, so I swear you'll never get bored.

FOR THE OATS

1 cup rolled oats

1 cup unsweetened almond milk

1 to 2 teaspoons honey or pure maple syrup

Pinch of sea salt

MIX-INS

2 tablespoons almond butter

½ banana, mashed

½ teaspoon pure vanilla extract

PICK SOME TOPPINGS

2 tablespoons chocolate chips

2 tablespoons blueberries

¼ cup slivered almonds

Sliced bananas

Drizzle of honey

Drizzle of almond butter

Pinch of bee pollen (if y'all wanna get weird with it)

1. In a small bowl, add the oats, almond milk, honey, and salt and stir to combine. Add any of the mix-ins you'd like and stir well.

2. Split the mixture between two mason jars or containers with a lid and refrigerate for at least 4 hours or overnight.

3. To serve, add on your favorite toppings and enjoy!

Good for Ya!

The Best Avocado Toast of All Time

MAKES 1 OR 2 SERVINGS

PREP TIME:
5 minutes

COOK TIME:
8 minutes

Y'all know I love toast. Most of the time I just do a little butter or jam for breakfast, but sometimes I want a little something more. If I have an avocado that's ripe and ready to eat, it's gotta be an avocado toast morning. First of all, forget your toaster. The best avocado toast you'll have is going to start out grilled in a pan with olive oil. Trust me, the flavor is one hundred times better. Then bring it all together with a little flaky salt, another drizzle of olive oil, and maybe a sprinkle of crushed red pepper flakes on your mashed avocado. This simple little avocado toast is actually packed with whole grains and healthy fats too, so it's a win-win!

½ teaspoon extra-virgin olive oil, plus more (optional) for serving

2 slices whole-grain bread

½ small avocado

½ teaspoon fresh lemon juice

⅛ teaspoon garlic powder

Pinch of sea salt, plus more for serving

⅛ teaspoon freshly ground black pepper

Pinch of crushed red pepper flakes, for serving (optional)

1. In a skillet, heat the oil over medium-high heat. Add the bread and reduce the heat to medium. Flip the bread to coat the other side in oil, then cook, flipping occasionally, until nice and toasty, 3 to 4 minutes per side. Transfer the toasts to paper towels.

2. In a small bowl, combine the avocado, lemon juice, garlic powder, salt, and pepper. Gently mash with the back of a fork.

3. Top the toasts with the mashed avocado mixture and drizzle with oil if you'd like. Sprinkle with sea salt and add pepper flakes if ya like it hot.

Sausage Egg Biscuit Casserole

MAKES 6 TO 8 SERVINGS

PREP TIME:
10 minutes

COOK TIME:
30 minutes

This hearty breakfast is for winners! I love sausage, bread, and cheese, so why not combine them? The finished dish is the most amazing combo of buttery biscuits, cheese, sausage, and egg, all in one bite. And the jam is really the cherry on top, so don't be afraid to go for it.

- 2 tablespoons extra-virgin olive oil
- 1 (10-count) can refrigerated buttermilk biscuit dough
- 1 (9.6-ounce) bag precooked sausage crumbles (I use Jimmy Dean)
- 1 cup shredded mozzarella cheese
- 1 cup shredded Cheddar cheese
- 8 large eggs, beaten
- 1 cup whole milk
- ¼ teaspoon salt
- ⅛ teaspoon freshly ground black pepper
- 1 teaspoon Tony Chachere's Creole Seasoning
- Red raspberry jam or your favorite jam, for serving

1. Preheat the oven to 425° F and grease a 9 x 13-inch baking dish with the oil.

2. Separate the biscuit dough and arrange it in the bottom of your baking dish. Firmly press and stretch the dough, pinching together any seams, until the bottom of the dish is completely covered. Top with the sausage crumbles and sprinkle with the mozzarella and Cheddar.

3. In a large bowl, whisk the eggs and milk until combined. Season with the salt, pepper, and Tony's seasoning. Whisk until frothy, then pour over the sausage and cheese in the baking dish.

4. Bake until the eggs are cooked through and a toothpick inserted in the center comes out clean, 25 to 30 minutes. If the casserole starts browning too quickly, cover with foil.

5. Slice into squares and serve hot. Let each person top it off with a good spread of their favorite jam.

French Kiss Toast

MAKES 4 SERVINGS

PREP TIME:
5 minutes

COOK TIME:
15 minutes

If French toast is on the menu, you better believe that's what my husband is going to order. Eric has two weaknesses when it comes to breakfast: doughnuts and French toast. I came up with this easy French toast recipe one morning and knew it was a hit when Eric gave me a full-mouth grin and a thumbs-up.

You can let your loaf of bread go stale for about 2 days before making the French toast or make it fresh—your choice. Stale bread will give you a sturdy crust; soft bread will give you a soft crust!

4 large eggs

¾ cup whole milk

1 teaspoon pure vanilla extract

1 teaspoon ground cinnamon

2 teaspoons sugar

Cooking spray, for the griddle

1 loaf French bread, sliced into eight 1-inch-thick slices

Powdered sugar, for serving

Pure maple syrup, warmed, for serving

1. In a medium bowl, beat the eggs, milk, vanilla, cinnamon, and sugar with a wire whisk until frothy. Transfer to a shallow dish and set aside.

2. Coat a griddle or large skillet with cooking spray and place over medium heat.

3. Working with two slices of bread at a time, dip the bread in the egg mixture until well coated on both sides. Place on the hot griddle. Cook, flipping, until golden, 1 to 2 minutes per side. Transfer to a plate and repeat with the remaining bread.

4. Serve this French toast "kissed" with a sprinkle of powdered sugar and your favorite maple syrup.

Mini Frittata Egg Muffins

MAKES 4 TO 6 SERVINGS

PREP TIME:
10 minutes

COOK TIME:
20 minutes

These mini frittatas are great for feeding a lot of people at one time. Whether it's a holiday breakfast, a baby or bridal shower brunch, or a big gathering after church, these yummy egg muffins are gonna be a hit. Plus, if you're trying to find healthy ways to meal prep, these little frittata muffins are a perfect filling, protein-packed breakfast (see note). I can eat a dozen myself, so make a double batch if you're like me!

Cooking spray, for the muffin tin

5 slices thick-cut bacon

12 large eggs

2 tablespoons heavy cream

½ teaspoon salt

¼ teaspoon freshly ground black pepper

2 cloves garlic, minced

½ cup shredded mozzarella cheese

½ cup shredded mild Cheddar cheese

3 to 4 mushrooms, sliced

½ red bell pepper, diced

2 tablespoons finely diced onion

1. Preheat the oven to 350°F. Coat a 12-cup muffin tin with cooking spray or line with silicone muffin cups.

2. In a large skillet over medium heat, cook the bacon until browned on the bottom, about 4 minutes. Flip with tongs and cook until browned and crispy, another 2 minutes. Transfer to a plate lined with paper towels. When the bacon is cool enough to handle, crumble it.

3. In a large bowl, whisk the eggs and heavy cream until the mixture is pale yellow and creamy. Season with the salt and pepper. Stir in the garlic, mozzarella, and Cheddar.

4. Divide the mushrooms, bell pepper, onion, and bacon among the muffin cups, then top off with some of the egg mixture to fill each cup.

5. Bake until the muffins are firm in the center and no longer jiggle, about 20 minutes. Let them cool in the muffin tin for a few minutes before removing to serve.

Jessie's note:

Feel free to mix it up with your fillings depending on what you have on hand in the fridge. Other egg muffin combos to try: chopped spinach, feta, and roasted red pepper; or sausage crumbles, sharp Cheddar, and chopped broccoli!

Louisiana Beignets

**MAKES ABOUT
20 BEIGNETS**

PREP TIME:
1 hour 20 minutes

COOK TIME:
20 minutes

I grew up eating beignets as if they were the standard doughnut. I didn't realize they are special to Louisiana, because they were such a constant in my life. These are my favorite doughnuts in the world, and I could eat ten of them. The smell of fried dough and powdered sugar all coming together gets me giddy thinking about it.

¾ cup lukewarm water

1 (¼-ounce) packet active dry yeast

⅓ cup plus 1 tablespoon granulated sugar

3½ to 4 cups bread flour, plus more for rolling

1 large egg, room temperature, and beaten

3 tablespoons salted butter, melted and cooled

½ cup evaporated milk

1 teaspoon pure vanilla extract

½ teaspoon salt

Vegetable oil, for the bowl and for frying

Powdered sugar, for dusting

1. In a small bowl, combine the lukewarm water, yeast, and 1 tablespoon sugar. Set aside to proof until frothy and bubbly, about 10 minutes.

2. To the bowl of a stand mixer fitted with the dough hook, add the yeast mixture, 2 cups flour, the remaining ⅓ cup sugar, the beaten egg, butter, evaporated milk, vanilla, and salt. Mix on low speed until combined. Add 1½ cups flour, ½ cup at a time, and continue mixing on low speed until a soft dough forms, 5 to 6 minutes. If the dough is still too sticky to work with, continue adding 2 tablespoons flour at a time, up to an additional ½ cup.

3. Lightly oil a large bowl. Form the beignet dough into a ball and add to the bowl, cover with plastic wrap, and let rise in a warm, dark place until doubled in size, at least 1 hour.

4. On a lightly floured work surface, roll the dough out about ⅓ inch thick. Cut into 2 x 2-inch squares.

5. Fill a Dutch oven or deep pot with enough oil to cover by 3 inches and heat to 370°F. Working in batches of two or three, fry the beignets until golden and puffy, 1 to 2 minutes on each side.

6. Transfer the beignets to a paper towel–lined plate and dust with a generous amount of powdered sugar. Serve warm.

Karen's Quiche

MAKES 2 QUICHES

PREP TIME:
15 minutes

COOK TIME:
35 minutes

Nothing says brunch like a beautiful quiche, and this one has it all. Veggies, meats, and four different cheeses, oh my! But what makes this quiche the best is the crust, and I'll say it throughout this book—nobody does piecrust like Marie Callender. My mama will tell you the same thing: This crust is the best to make the perfect quiche every time. Keep a few empty crusts and some chopped broccoli in the freezer so you can whip one up for a special breakfast on a moment's notice.

2 tablespoons extra-virgin olive oil

½ white onion, thinly sliced

1 cup diced ham or bacon

1 (4-ounce) can mushrooms, drained

Kosher salt and freshly ground black pepper

¼ teaspoon Tony Chachere's Creole Seasoning

10 large eggs

1 cup whole milk

2 tablespoons chopped scallions

1 (2-count) package frozen piecrusts, thawed (I use Marie Callender's)

½ cup shredded Swiss cheese

⅓ cup shredded Parmesan cheese

1 cup frozen chopped broccoli, thawed

½ cup shredded Italian cheese blend

⅓ cup shredded Cheddar cheese

Sliced mixed fruit, for serving

1. Preheat the oven to 350°F.

2. In a large skillet, heat the oil over medium heat. Add the white onion and sauté until translucent, 5 to 7 minutes. Add the ham and mushrooms and cook just until heated through, 2 to 3 minutes. Season lightly with salt, pepper, and the Tony's seasoning. Remove from the heat.

3. In a large bowl, whisk together the eggs, milk, and scallions until frothy. Set aside.

4. Press the piecrusts into two 9-inch pie plates and place on a baking sheet.

5. Sprinkle each piecrust with half the Swiss and Parmesan cheeses. Divide the broccoli and the ham mixture between the crusts, then pour half the egg mixture into each crust. Top each with half the Italian cheese blend and half the Cheddar cheese. Season with pepper.

6. Bake the quiches until golden and the center no longer jiggles, about 35 minutes. Serve warm with a side of mixed fruit.

Waffles

MAKES 4 TO 6 SERVINGS

PREP TIME:
10 minutes

COOK TIME:
15 minutes

When I bring out the waffle maker, my whole family gets excited because it doesn't happen on a weekly basis like pancakes or scrambled eggs. Nope, these are special-occasion waffles that are perfect for a lazy Sunday morning. Once the batter is made, everyone waits patiently around the waffle iron, ready to get the next hot one—and they are devoured almost before the next batch is ready! Serve these with warm maple syrup and a side of crispy bacon and watch them disappear.

2 cups all-purpose flour

2 tablespoons sugar

2 teaspoons baking powder

1 teaspoon sea salt

2 large eggs

1½ cups whole milk

⅓ cup unsalted butter, melted and cooled, plus more for serving

1 tablespoon pure vanilla extract

Cooking spray or avocado oil, for the waffle iron

Pure maple syrup, warmed, for serving

Bacon, for serving

1. Preheat the waffle iron to medium.

2. In a large bowl, combine the flour, sugar, baking powder, and salt. Stir well to get out any clumps.

3. In a medium bowl, whisk together the eggs, milk, butter, and vanilla. Add to the flour mixture and whisk to combine.

4. Coat the hot waffle iron with cooking spray or grease with a little avocado oil to prevent the waffles from sticking. Scoop about ½ cup of the batter (depending on your waffle iron) into the waffle iron and close the lid. Cook for 3 to 5 minutes or until lightly golden brown, transfer to a plate, and repeat with the remaining batter. Serve the waffles hot with warm maple syrup and butter and bacon alongside.

Monte Cristo

MAKES 1 SANDWICH

PREP TIME:
10 minutes

COOK TIME:
8 minutes

If a Monte Cristo is on the menu, all bets are off. What's not to love? Meat, cheese, bread, jam, powdered sugar, butter? Ahhhhh—the French did this recipe right. Monte Cristo recipes are all pretty much the same, but here's my version.

3 tablespoons salted butter

3 slices French toast–style bread or other thick bread

1 teaspoon Dijon mustard

½ cup strawberry jam, plus more for serving

2 slices Swiss cheese

2 slices thick-cut honey ham

2 slices honey turkey

1 tablespoon extra-virgin olive oil

1 large egg, lightly beaten

1 tablespoon unsweetened almond milk or milk of your choice

Pinch of sea salt

Pinch of ground cinnamon

Powdered sugar, for dusting

1. Using 1 tablespoon butter, lightly butter one side of two slices of the bread and both sides of the third (inner) slice.

2. Place the first two slices of bread on a plate butter side down. Spread the Dijon mustard on one slice of bread. Spread 1 teaspoon strawberry jam on the other slice. These are your bottom and top sandwich pieces.

3. Build your sandwich in this order: 1 slice of Swiss on top of the Dijon, followed by the ham, then the inner slice of bread. Next add the turkey, followed by the remaining slice of Swiss and the remaining slice of bread, jelly side down. Use a spatula to gently flatten the sandwich.

4. When ready to fry, in a skillet, heat the oil and remaining 2 tablespoons butter over medium-high heat.

5. In a shallow dish, whisk together the egg, milk, salt, and cinnamon. Carefully dip the sandwich into the egg mixture to coat each side.

6. Add the sandwich to the hot pan and cook until the bread is golden and the cheese is melted, 3 to 4 minutes per side. Transfer to paper towels and pat dry.

7. Dust the sandwich with powdered sugar, slice in half, and serve with more jam on the side.

London Fog Tea

MAKES 2 SERVINGS

PREP TIME:
5 minutes

When I was pregnant with Forrest, I had the weirdest aversion to the smell and taste of coffee. This lasted for the first three months of my pregnancy. If you know me you know I love coffee more than anything. I could drink it all day long like a little old lady. I wake up thinking about coffee, and I need the caffeine to stay like a little Energizer Bunny. My aversion was so bad that just the smell of coffee made me want to puke—and I'm pretty sure I did a couple of times. I wouldn't even let Eric brew it. But I still desperately needed that caffeine, so I did my research and came upon the London Fog. It was so comforting and delicious and gave me the tiny bit of caffeine I needed to start my day. From time to time, I still will make one, and it reminds me of my growing baby Forrest.

2 teaspoons loose Earl Grey tea (or 2 Earl Grey tea bags)

2 cups boiling water

¾ cup whole milk

2 tablespoons honey or pure maple syrup

1 teaspoon pure vanilla extract

1. Place the loose tea (or tea bags) in a large mason jar. Pour the boiling water over the tea and let steep for 5 minutes.

2. Strain the tea using a fine-mesh sieve (or remove the tea bags). Divide between two mugs.

3. Add the milk, honey, and vanilla to a milk frother and froth until velvety and frothy. Divide between the two mugs of tea and serve.

Ooey-Gooey Almond Butter Banana Bread

MAKES 8 TO 10 SERVINGS

PREP TIME:
15 minutes

COOK TIME:
1 hour

This might be the best banana bread I've ever made. It's got it all: tons of chocolate chips, sweet and salty swirls of almond butter, and a hint of maple. This bread is so soft and moist that you'll think you're eating dessert—it's that good!

Cooking spray, for the loaf pan

1/3 cup pure maple syrup

8 tablespoons (1 stick) unsalted butter, melted, plus more for serving

2 large eggs

1 tablespoon pure vanilla extract

2 large overripe bananas, mashed

1/2 cup brown sugar

1 1/2 cups white whole wheat flour or all-purpose flour

1 1/2 teaspoons baking soda

3/4 teaspoon salt

1/2 cup semisweet chocolate chips, plus more (optional) for sprinkling

1/2 cup creamy almond butter

Honey, for serving

1. Preheat the oven to 350°F. Coat a 9 x 5-inch loaf pan with cooking spray and line with parchment paper.

2. In a large bowl, whisk together the maple syrup, butter, eggs, vanilla, bananas, and sugar until well combined. Beat in the flour, baking soda, and salt until just combined.

3. Stir in the chocolate chips, then add the almond butter in teaspoon-size dollops and gently swirl it through the batter.

4. Pour the batter into the prepared loaf pan and sprinkle with more chocolate chips if you'd like. Bake until set in the center, 50 to 60 minutes. If the bread begins to brown too quickly, tent with aluminum foil. Remove from the oven and let cool for at least 30 minutes before slicing.

5. Serve with warm butter and honey spread on top and watch it melt into the gooey yumminess.

Southern Buttermilk Biscuits

MAKES ABOUT 12 BISCUITS

PREP TIME:
20 minutes

COOK TIME:
20 minutes

Buttermilk biscuits are one of those sides that goes with just about anything, and, believe it or not, they are one of the easier breads to make! It's all about working your dough *juuust* enough to make the biscuits rise without getting tough. You don't want to work it like pizza dough or knead it too much, but just enough. After you make these once, they'll become a weekly staple. Serve them hot with butter and jam or alongside a big plate of homemade fried chicken.

2 cups self-rising flour, plus more for the surface

1½ tablespoons sugar

⅓ cup shortening

1 cup buttermilk

3 tablespoons unsalted butter, melted, plus more (optional) for serving

Jam or jelly, for serving (optional)

Honey, for drizzling (optional)

1. Preheat the oven to 350°F.

2. In a large bowl, whisk together the flour and sugar until combined. Cut in the shortening with a pastry cutter or fork until the mixture resembles coarse sand. Pour in the buttermilk and stir until a dough forms.

3. Turn the dough out onto a floured surface and knead until no longer sticky, about 4 to 6 folds (see note).

4. Roll or press the dough out into a 1-inch-thick round, then use a biscuit cutter or the end of a mason jar (which is what I do) to cut out the biscuits. Re-form the dough scraps and repeat the cutting process until most of the dough is used.

5. Arrange the biscuits on a baking sheet and bake until golden brown, 15 to 20 minutes. Halfway through baking, brush the tops of the biscuits with the melted butter.

6. Serve with your favorite jam or jelly or with butter and a drizzle of honey.

Jessie's note:

You can save half the dough and freeze it in a plastic bag or refrigerate for up to 3 days before baking.

Monkey Bread

MAKES 6 TO
8 SERVINGS

PREP TIME:
20 minutes

COOK TIME:
45 minutes

A friend of mine made this for Easter brunch back in the day, and I never forgot it. I had never had monkey bread before, and I remember being kind of upset about that. How had I been without this yummy, doughy, cinnamony, fluffy deliciousness my whole life? Here is my take on it, which is the easy shortcut version so you can get right to eating it if you have no patience when it comes to sweets like me—I want it now!

This is the perfect dish to bring to a gathering because it's very interactive and feeds lots of folks.

2 sticks (8 ounces) unsalted butter, plus more for greasing the pan

1 cup granulated sugar

2 teaspoons ground cinnamon

2 (8-count) cans refrigerated buttermilk biscuit dough

½ cup chopped pecans (optional)

1 cup firmly packed brown sugar

1. Preheat the oven to 350°F and lightly grease a Bundt pan with butter. In a large plastic bag, mix the granulated sugar and cinnamon and set aside.

2. Separate the biscuit dough into 16 biscuits and cut each into quarters. Working in batches, add the biscuit dough to the cinnamon sugar bag and shake to coat. Arrange in the prepared pan, alternating layers of pecans (if using) and biscuit dough. Refrigerate while you make the sauce.

3. In a medium saucepan, melt the 2 sticks of butter over medium-high heat. Add the brown sugar and cook, stirring, until completely dissolved, 2 to 3 minutes. Pour the mixture over the biscuits in the pan. Bake until golden brown, 30 to 40 minutes. Let cool in the pan for about 10 minutes.

4. To serve, place a large plate or serving platter on top of the monkey bread and, while holding both the pan and the plate, turn upside down. Remove the Bundt pan to reveal the monkey bread. Let your guests pull apart pieces to enjoy!

2

I love me some apps! Appetizers are just as important as the main course, in my opinion. I love the smaller portions and the variety of flavors, so you hit every taste bud before the main course. Whether we're at a restaurant and I'm wanting to try a tasty new app (I always order too many—LOL) or I'm at home cooking dinner, an appetizer is always a must for me. Dinner with the fam is always like a dinner party, so I treat every meal that way! As I'm cooking, I make sure to feed everyone little bites as we prepare to sit down as a family. Here are some of my favorite family appetizers that I know y'all are going to love.

For Starters

Maple Bacon-Wrapped Shrimp

MAKES ABOUT 20 SHRIMP

PREP TIME:
10 minutes

COOK TIME:
18 minutes

Bacon and shrimp are an appetizer match made in heaven. You've got a salty slice of thick-cut bacon wrapped around tender, juicy shrimp, topped off with a hint of sweet and spicy maple glaze that is so addicting. Anytime I make these for a get-together, they are the first thing that's gone and they're always a hit.

1 pound shrimp (about 20), peeled and deveined, tails on

10 slices thick-cut maple bacon, each cut in half

2 tablespoons unsalted butter, melted

2 tablespoons pure maple syrup

⅛ teaspoon garlic powder

Pinch of chili powder

2 tablespoons chopped parsley

Pinch of freshly ground black pepper

1. Preheat the oven to 400°F and line a large baking sheet with aluminum foil.

2. Wrap each piece of shrimp with a piece of bacon and secure with a toothpick. Arrange the shrimp in a single layer on the prepared sheet.

3. In a small bowl, stir together the butter, maple syrup, garlic powder, and chili powder. Transfer half the glaze to a separate small bowl. Brush the wrapped shrimp with half the glaze. Bake until the bacon is crisp and the shrimp is pink and cooked through, 18 minutes.

4. Using a clean brush, coat the shrimp with the remaining maple butter glaze. Sprinkle with the parsley and some pepper.

Deviled Eggs

MAKES
24 DEVILED EGGS

PREP TIME:
15 minutes

In Tennessee you will find deviled eggs on the menu at most Southern-style restaurants. They're a crowd-pleasing staple, perfect for all the holidays. I typically whip these up for Easter brunch or a church function. It just feels right, ya know?

1 dozen hard-boiled large eggs, peeled

⅓ cup mayonnaise

1 tablespoon yellow mustard

1 tablespoon dried dill

1 to 2 dashes Louisiana hot sauce

Sea salt and freshly ground black pepper

¼ teaspoon garlic powder

½ teaspoon Tony Chachere's Creole Seasoning

¼ cup bacon jam (optional; see note)

1 teaspoon paprika, for garnish

1. Pat the eggs dry with paper towels and slice in half. Transfer the yolks to a medium bowl and arrange the whites on a plate or platter.

2. Mash the yolks with a fork. Add the mayo, mustard, dill, and hot sauce and stir until smooth (some small chunks are OK). Season with salt, pepper, the garlic powder, and Tony's seasoning.

3. Using a spoon, scoop some of the yolk filling into each egg white half. Top each with ½ teaspoon bacon jam (if using). Garnish with the paprika to serve.

Jessie's note:

You can find bacon jam in your local grocery store or online specialty shops.

Classic Cheese Board

**MAKES 6 TO
8 SERVINGS**

PREP TIME:
20 minutes

Whenever folks come over, I love to put out a huge spread. Everyone thinks it took so much time and effort, but the trick is all in the presentation. My go-to cheese board is so simple: cheese, olives, some crackers and bread, honey, and little pantry odds and ends. It takes no time at all but always looks impressive (and it tastes good).

First, use wooden cheese boards or serving platters of different sizes and textures. This creates a look and feel of abundance. Then head to the pantry and gather your favorite crackers, spreads or jams, honey, dried fruit, and nuts. Balance your pantry goods with two or three cheeses that vary in texture. Arrange everything on your boards, keep the wine flowin', and your guests will always think it's a big deal!

1 (6-ounce) wedge Parmesan cheese

1 (8-ounce) wheel triple-cream brie cheese

1 (6-ounce) wedge Sartori Merlot BellaVitano cheese

3 ounces prosciutto

4 ounces sliced cured sausage

1 cup Marcona almonds

6 ounces pitted olives

1 sleeve golden round crackers (about 30 crackers)

1 baguette, sliced into rounds

2 to 3 sprigs fresh rosemary

1 (12-ounce) bottle honey, for serving

1 (8.5-ounce) jar fig jam, for serving

DESTIN DIPPING OIL

¼ cup extra-virgin olive oil

¼ teaspoon garlic powder

½ teaspoon dried basil

¼ teaspoon onion powder

½ teaspoon fresh lemon juice

2 teaspoons grated Parmesan cheese

Sea salt and freshly ground black pepper

1. Arrange the cheeses, meats, almonds, olives, crackers, and bread on a cheese board or large serving platter. Arrange the rosemary sprigs decoratively around the board or platter.

2. Make the dipping oil: Add the oil, garlic powder, basil, onion powder, lemon juice, and Parmesan to a small serving bowl, season with salt and pepper, and stir well to combine. Place on the board if there's room or serve on the side.

3. To serve, drizzle honey over the brie and add the jars of jam and honey to the board.

Cajun Snack Mix

MAKES ABOUT
9 CUPS

PREP TIME:
10 minutes

COOK TIME:
1 hour

Who doesn't love a good old-fashioned snack mix? It's perfect for holiday parties or get-togethers when you need something to set out for an appetizer. This is a twist on your basic Chex mix with a little Cajun kick! Adjust the spice up or down depending on your guests, or make a double batch with one a little more caliente and the other more kid-friendly.

2 cups each Corn Chex, Rice Chex, and Wheat Chex

1 cup pretzels

1 cup mixed nuts

1 cup oyster crackers or Goldfish crackers

8 tablespoons (1 stick) unsalted butter, melted

7 to 10 shakes hot sauce

2 tablespoons Worcestershire sauce

1 to 2 teaspoons Tony Chachere's Creole Seasoning

½ teaspoon smoked paprika

¼ teaspoon garlic powder

¼ teaspoon onion powder

1. Preheat the oven to 300°F.

2. Add the cereals, pretzels, nuts, and crackers to a large bowl.

3. In a medium bowl, stir together the melted butter, hot sauce, Worcestershire, Tony's seasoning, paprika, garlic powder, and onion powder. Take a piece of the dry mix, dip it in, and give it a taste. Adjust the heat and spices to your liking.

4. Pour the seasoned butter mixture over the dry mix and stir to coat. Spread on a baking sheet and bake until golden brown, about 1 hour, stirring every 15 minutes. Let cool before serving or portioning into plastic bags to store (or share).

Cheesy Baked Bean Dip

MAKES 6 SERVINGS

PREP TIME:
10 minutes

COOK TIME:
30 minutes

This recipe is as delicious as it is simple. All it takes is five ingredients and a little time in the oven, and you've got a gooey, cheesy baked bean dip that will have everyone you know begging for the recipe. It's perfect for game days, holidays, or anytime you need something hot and cheesy!

2 (15.5-ounce) cans pinto beans, rinsed and drained

4 ounces cream cheese, softened

½ cup sour cream

2 tablespoons taco seasoning mix

1½ cups shredded Mexican cheese blend

Optional toppings: sliced scallions, salsa, hot sauce

Tortilla chips, for serving

1. Preheat the oven to 350°F. Add the beans to a large bowl and mash with a potato masher or the back of a large spoon until softened and breaking apart.

2. Add the cream cheese, sour cream, taco seasoning, and ½ cup cheese and stir well to combine. Transfer to an 8 x 8-inch baking dish and top with the remaining cheese. Bake until the dip is bubbly and the cheese is golden, 20 to 30 minutes. Garnish with any of the optional toppings you'd like and serve hot with tortilla chips.

Pigs in a Huddled Blanket

MAKES 48 PIECES

PREP TIME:
15 minutes

COOK TIME:
20 minutes

I love hosting guests and I love making yummy appetizers and meals for everyone to enjoy. I used to grab frozen pigs in a blanket from the grocery store, throw them in the oven, and lay them out, but when I realized how easy it is to make them myself (and how much better they taste!), that was a game changer. These bake all snuggled up next to one another, so they'll stick together slightly. When you serve them, people can just pull them off the platter. They'll pull away easily and are ready for dipping into Dijon or just eating all on their own.

2 (8-ounce) packages crescent roll dough (I use Pillsbury)

3 tablespoons unsalted butter, melted

2 (14-ounce) packages cocktail franks

1 tablespoon Italian seasoning

1 teaspoon garlic powder

Salt and freshly ground black pepper

Dijon mustard, for serving

1. Preheat the oven to 375°F and line a baking sheet with parchment paper.

2. Unroll the crescent roll dough onto a clean work surface and brush all over with some of the melted butter. Pull apart the crescent triangles and cut each one into thirds to make three skinny triangles. Place a cocktail frank on the long side of each triangle and roll up.

3. Arrange the rolled-up piggies on the prepared baking sheet in two concentric circles, letting them touch one another. Brush with more melted butter and sprinkle with the Italian seasoning, garlic powder, and a pinch each of salt and pepper. Bake until golden brown, 15 to 20 minutes.

4. Serve the piggies warm with Dijon mustard for dipping.

Smoked Tuna Dip

MAKES 6 TO 8 SERVINGS

PREP TIME: 1 hour 5 minutes

I love me some tuna dip in the summer, with saltines, hot sauce, and a cold beer. That's just the girl on the coast in me. This is my basic recipe, but when you're putting it together, I recommend tasting and seasoning as you go. If you like it extra spicy, you can add more hot sauce or an extra dash of Tony's seasoning on top to serve.

5 ounces cream cheese, softened

½ cup low-fat mayonnaise

3 tablespoons chopped dill pickle

1 (8-ounce) tin yellowfin tuna packed in water, drained

½ teaspoon liquid smoke

1 teaspoon hot sauce (I prefer Louisiana brand)

1 teaspoon paprika

1 teaspoon garlic powder

1 teaspoon Tony Chachere's Creole Seasoning

Saltine crackers, for serving

1. In a large bowl, stir together the cream cheese, mayonnaise, dill pickle, tuna, liquid smoke, hot sauce, paprika, garlic powder, and Tony's seasoning until well combined. Divide among a few mason jars, cover, and refrigerate for 1 hour to let the flavors meld.

2. Serve in the mason jars with lots of saltines!

Fried Eggplant

MAKES 4 TO 6 SERVINGS

PREP TIME:
10 minutes

COOK TIME:
18 minutes

There are a couple veggies that are just better fried, and, y'all, eggplant is one of them. I love the combo of crispy seasoned bread crumbs and salty Parmesan cheese. This is such a great appetizer or side, and it's so easy to make at home. Serve with a drizzle of good olive oil and some fresh basil.

½ cup all-purpose flour

1 large egg, beaten

¼ teaspoon sea salt

Pinch of black pepper

1½ cups Italian bread crumbs

½ cup grated Parmesan cheese, plus more for serving

2 garlic cloves, finely minced

1 tablespoon Italian seasoning

1 large eggplant, sliced into ¼-inch-thick rounds

Extra-virgin olive oil, for frying and serving

2 tablespoons chopped fresh parsley, for serving

Marinara sauce, for serving

1. Add the flour to a shallow bowl. Add the beaten egg to a second shallow bowl and season with the salt and pepper. In a third shallow bowl, combine the Italian bread crumbs, Parmesan, garlic, and Italian seasoning.

2. Dredge the eggplant slices in the flour, then in the beaten egg, and then in the bread crumb mixture. Arrange on a baking sheet.

3. In a large skillet, heat ¼ inch oil over medium-high heat. Once the oil is hot (about 350°F), working in batches of 3 or 4, fry the eggplant until golden brown on each side, about 3 minutes total. Transfer to a plate lined with paper towels.

4. Serve the fried eggplant hot, topped with Parmesan, parsley, marinara sauce, and a drizzle of oil.

Cheddar Biscuits

MAKES 12 BISCUITS

PREP TIME:
15 minutes

COOK TIME:
15 minutes

With these biscuits, if you know, you know. They are so buttery and soft, with a hit of garlic and that secret blend of seasonings that make them irresistible—except now it's not a secret anymore! Here's how I copycat the famous Red Lobster Cheddar Bay Biscuits from scratch.

FOR THE
BISCUITS

2 cups all-purpose
flour

1 teaspoon sugar

2 teaspoons baking
powder

½ teaspoon baking
soda

1 teaspoon garlic
powder

½ teaspoon salt

¼ teaspoon Old Bay
Seasoning

1 cup buttermilk

8 tablespoons
(1 stick) unsalted
butter, melted and
cooled

1 cup shredded
Cheddar cheese

FOR THE
GARLIC BUTTER
TOPPING

4 tablespoons
(½ stick) unsalted
butter, melted

1 teaspoon garlic
powder

1 teaspoon dried
parsley

½ teaspoon onion
powder

1. Preheat the oven to 425°F and line a baking sheet with parchment paper.

2. Make the biscuits: In a large bowl, combine the flour, sugar, baking powder, baking soda, garlic powder, salt, and Old Bay. In a separate bowl, whisk together the buttermilk and melted butter.

3. Add the wet ingredients to the dry ingredients and stir until the dough lumpy but well mixed. Fold in the Cheddar (do not overmix).

4. Arrange ¼-cup portions of dough on the prepared baking sheet. Bake until golden brown, 10 to 15 minutes.

5. While the biscuits bake, make the garlic butter: In a small bowl, combine the melted butter, garlic powder, parsley, and onion powder. Brush onto the biscuits before serving.

3

A salad is like a bowl full of endless possibilities. There are so many different combinations you can come up with that I swear I never get bored! I'm not talking about limp lettuce and a pile of shredded cheese covered in ranch—oh, no. I love mixing it up with different fruits for a sweet and savory combo like peaches and goat cheese, or adding different textures in my Chinese chicken salad.

No Boring Salads

Recipes with ○ icon indicate "Good for Ya!" recipes.

Caesar Salad by Yours Truly

MAKES 4 SERVINGS

PREP TIME:
15 minutes

I love Caesar salad, but I won't touch it if there are anchovies—ha! This recipe is anchovy-free, so for the three people I've ever known in my life who want the dead little fishes on top, I'm sorry this one doesn't have them. I like this recipe because the romaine leaves aren't torn. It feels fancier this way, with the whole leaves all laid out on the plate. I had a salad like this at a restaurant, and the added Worcestershire drizzle made it even better. Hope y'all like it, because it's damn good.

FOR THE SALAD

2 romaine hearts, washed and patted dry, leaves separated

2 tablespoons extra-virgin olive oil

Salt and freshly ground black pepper

¼ teaspoon garlic powder

Juice of ½ lemon

½ teaspoon Worcestershire sauce

1 cup freshly shaved Parmesan cheese

1 cup seasoned croutons

FOR THE DRESSING

¼ cup extra-virgin olive oil

Juice of ½ lemon

2 cloves garlic, crushed

1 teaspoon Dijon mustard

½ teaspoon Worcestershire sauce

1 cup olive oil mayonnaise

3 tablespoons freshly grated Parmesan cheese

Sea salt and freshly ground black pepper

1. Make the salad: Place the romaine leaves in a large wooden bowl. Drizzle with the oil and toss to coat. Season with a good pinch of salt, several grinds of pepper, and the garlic powder and toss again. Add the lemon juice and Worcestershire and toss once more. Taste and adjust seasonings to your liking.

2. Make the dressing: In a medium bowl, whisk together the oil, lemon juice, garlic, Dijon, and Worcestershire. Add the mayonnaise and grated Parmesan, season with salt and pepper, and whisk until well combined.

3. To serve the salad, divide the romaine leaves among plates, drizzle with the dressing, and top with the shaved Parmesan and croutons.

Chinese Chicken Salad

MAKES 4 TO 6 SERVINGS

PREP TIME: 15 minutes

I was at a photo shoot once and the caterer kept bringing around all these delicious snacks. One of the evening snacks was a Chinese chicken salad served in a mini to-go carton. It was delicious—I've never forgotten that tangy, crunchy bite and how satisfying it was. Now I make my best version of the salad at home. I like to serve it with chopsticks and cute little Chinese to-go cartons I found on Amazon to make it festive and fun. Side note: Feel free to garnish with sesame seeds and use sesame oil, but because of a bad allergy in the Decker house, I avoid them!

FOR THE SALAD

- 4 cups finely shredded green or Napa cabbage
- 1½ cups finely shredded red cabbage
- 1 cup shredded carrots
- 1 cup mandarin orange sections
- ¼ cup shelled edamame
- ¼ cup sliced scallions, plus more for garnish
- 3 cups chopped rotisserie chicken
- ⅓ cup slivered almonds, toasted
- 1 cup wonton strips

FOR THE DRESSING

- 3 tablespoons extra-virgin olive oil or grapeseed oil
- ¼ cup rice vinegar
- ¼ cup hoisin sauce
- 1½ tablespoons soy sauce
- 1 teaspoon honey
- 1 teaspoon finely grated peeled fresh ginger

1. Make the salad: Add the green cabbage, red cabbage, carrots, mandarin oranges, edamame, scallions, chicken, and almonds to a large bowl. Toss to combine.

2. Make the dressing: In a small bowl, whisk together the olive oil, vinegar, hoisin, soy sauce, honey, and ginger until well combined.

3. Pour the dressing over the salad and toss to coat. Sprinkle with the wonton strips and garnish with sliced scallions. Serve immediately.

Peach and Goat Cheese Salad

MAKES 4 SERVINGS

PREP TIME:
20 minutes

If you know me, you know I love peaches. Peach pie, peach cobbler, and, of course, peach and goat cheese salad! It's so naturally flavorful and juicy, the sweet peaches combining perfectly with crunchy pecans and creamy goat cheese. Serve this as a side or make it a meal with grilled chicken breast.

⅓ cup extra-virgin olive oil

2 tablespoons white wine vinegar

Salt and freshly ground black pepper

¼ teaspoon garlic powder

6 ounces mixed greens (about 4 cups)

½ cup chopped fresh basil

4 peaches, unpeeled and cut into chunks

1 tablespoon honey

1 cup sliced yellow grape tomatoes

½ cup crumbled goat cheese

1 cup pecan halves

½ small red onion, sliced

1. In a large bowl, whisk together the oil and vinegar. Season with salt, pepper, and the garlic powder. Add the mixed greens and basil and toss to coat in the dressing. In a separate bowl, toss the peaches with the honey to coat.

2. To serve, place the mixed greens on a large platter. Top with the honey peaches, tomatoes, crumbled goat cheese, pecans, and red onion.

Go-To Mexican Chopped Salad

MAKES 4 SERVINGS

PREP TIME:
20 minutes

Sometimes salads can seem boring, but not in my house. I love whipping up my own dressing and adding lots of different flavors and textures with toppings. This one is a full meal all on its own with protein-packed black beans, but you can bump up the protein even more by adding grilled shrimp or chicken.

FOR THE DRESSING

- ¼ cup fresh cilantro
- ¼ cup plain Greek yogurt or sour cream
- 1 clove garlic
- 1 tablespoon fresh lime juice
- ½ teaspoon honey
- ¼ teaspoon sea salt
- ¼ teaspoon ground cumin
- 2 tablespoons extra-virgin olive oil

FOR THE SALAD

- 1 head romaine lettuce, inner leaves only, chopped
- 1 (15-ounce) can black beans, rinsed and drained
- 2 Roma tomatoes, chopped
- 1 cup corn kernels
- 1 large avocado, halved, pitted, and diced
- 1 small red onion, diced
- ½ cup queso fresca or cotija cheese
- ½ cup chopped fresh cilantro, for garnish

1. Make the dressing: Add the cilantro, yogurt, garlic, lime juice, honey, salt, and cumin to a blender or food processor and pulse to combine. With the machine running, stream in the oil until the dressing emulsifies.

2. Make the salad: Divide the lettuce, black beans, chopped tomatoes, corn, avocado, red onion, and cheese among four bowls. Garnish with the chopped cilantro and drizzle the dressing on top.

Grilled Chicken Cobb Salad

MAKES 3 TO 4 SERVINGS

PREP TIME:
20 minutes

COOK TIME:
8 minutes

Here's another salad that I will make on repeat because it's so full of flavor and filling while also being pretty healthy. I love Cobb salad, but only when I make it myself. I want my chicken grilled and juicy, my dressing nice and creamy, and all the veggies crisp and fresh. No limp lettuce! When all the ingredients come together, it's the most amazing combo that leaves you feeling satisfied while getting in those healthy proteins and veggies!

4 chicken breasts

1 teaspoon sea salt

1 teaspoon freshly ground black pepper

Avocado oil

2 heads romaine lettuce, inner leaves only, chopped

1 cup cherry tomatoes, halved

1 cup chopped cucumber

4 hard-boiled large eggs, quartered

6 slices cooked bacon, chopped

1 medium avocado, halved, pitted, and diced

½ red onion, thinly sliced

2 ears grilled corn, kernels removed from the cob

FOR THE DRESSING

1 cup avocado mayonnaise

¼ cup whole milk

2 tablespoons white wine vinegar

2 tablespoons fresh dill, plus more for garnish

1 teaspoon garlic powder

½ teaspoon onion powder

1 teaspoon kosher or sea salt

½ teaspoon freshly ground black pepper

1. Preheat a grill to 350°F or place a grill pan over medium-high heat.

2. Season the chicken with the salt and pepper.

3. Brush the grill or pan with avocado oil. Add the chicken to the grill or grill pan and cook until it reaches an internal temperature of 165°F, 3 to 4 minutes on each side.

4. Make the dressing: Combine the mayonnaise, milk, vinegar, dill, garlic powder, onion powder, salt, and pepper in a bowl and whisk to combine. Refrigerate while you cook the chicken.

5. Remove the chicken from the grill or grill pan and let rest for 2 to 3 minutes before slicing.

6. To assemble the salad, layer the lettuce, chicken, tomatoes, cucumber, eggs, bacon, avocado, onion, and corn in a large serving bowl.

7. To serve, drizzle with the dressing, toss, and garnish with fresh dill.

4

It was so hard to figure out what to call this chapter, and then it hit me: "Hot in a Pot," because that's what each recipe is all about. It's those warm and comforting foods that cook on the stovetop in your biggest pot. Soups, stews, chilis, and even my chicken thigh bake! It's all in the pot.

Hot in a Pot

Recipes with ○ icon indicate "Good for Ya!" recipes.

Lentil Soup for the Soul

MAKES 4 SERVINGS

PREP TIME:
15 minutes

COOK TIME:
1 hour

Low in Calories, high in protein and vitamins, full of fiber, and FILLING . . . need I say more?

When I'm cutting back but want to feel full and get all the proper nutrition, this is my go-to soup. It's so delicious you'll be licking the bowl clean.

2 tablespoons extra-virgin olive oil

½ yellow onion, diced

2 cups sliced Yukon Gold potatoes

2 cups diced carrots

1 cup diced celery

2 cloves garlic, minced

8 cups chicken or vegetable broth

1 bay leaf

½ teaspoon dried thyme

1 teaspoon garlic powder

Tony Chachere's Creole Seasoning

Salt and freshly ground black pepper

2 cups dry green or black lentils

3 to 4 handfuls fresh spinach

Shaved Parmesan cheese, for serving

1. In a large pot or Dutch oven, heat the oil over medium heat. Add the onion and cook, stirring occasionally, until softened, about 3 minutes.

2. Add the potatoes, carrots, and celery and cook, stirring occasionally, until the celery is softened and the onion begins to caramelize, 7 to 10 minutes. Add the garlic and cook, stirring, until fragrant, 2 to 3 minutes.

3. Add the broth to the pot along with the bay leaf, thyme, and garlic powder. Season with Tony's seasoning, salt, and pepper to taste. Add the lentils, increase the heat to medium-high, and bring to a gentle simmer. Use a spoon to remove any frothy residue from the surface, then reduce the heat to medium-low, cover, and cook until the lentils are tender, 30 to 40 minutes.

4. Remove the bay leaf and stir in the spinach to wilt. Season with salt and pepper and ladle into bowls. Sprinkle with shaved Parmesan.

Meaty and Mighty Chili

MAKES 6 TO 8 SERVINGS

PREP TIME:
10 minutes

COOK TIME:
1 hour

I make tons of variations on chili because it's one of my staple dishes. I love the meat, I love the beans, and I love the flavors combined. I always feel so satisfied after! This might be my favorite chili recipe of all the ones I make—it's the perfect combination of traditional chili mixed with that hint of sweetness and spice. This is the kids' favorite version too, and they request it weekly. Trust me, you're going to love it.

2 tablespoons extra-virgin olive oil

1 small yellow onion, diced

1 red bell pepper, diced

1 green bell pepper, diced

2 cloves garlic, minced

2½ pounds ground beef

Salt and freshly ground black pepper

3 (15.5-ounce) cans red kidney beans, with their liquid

2 (15-ounce) cans tomato sauce

1 (10-ounce) can diced tomatoes with green chilis (you can use mild or original)

2 tablespoons ketchup

2 teaspoons Worcestershire sauce

1 tablespoon garlic powder

2 teaspoons brown sugar

1 teaspoon chili powder

1 teaspoon ground cumin

1 bay leaf

Cooked white rice, for serving

Shredded Cheddar cheese, for serving

Tortilla chips, for serving

1. In a large pot, heat the oil over medium-high heat. Add the onion, bell peppers, and garlic and cook, stirring, until the veggies begin to soften, 3 to 5 minutes.

2. Add the ground beef, season with salt and pepper, and cook breaking up the meat with a wooden spoon, until no longer pink, 12 to 15 minutes

3. Add the kidney beans, tomato sauce, diced tomatoes, ketchup, Worcestershire, garlic powder, brown sugar, chili powder, cumin, and bay leaf. Stir to combine. Bring the chili to a simmer.

4. Reduce the heat to low, cover partially, and cook 30 to 45 minutes or until the chili is thickened and the beans are soft.

5. When ready to serve, remove the bay leaf and ladle into bowls over white rice. Top with shredded Cheddar and serve with tortilla chips.

Pumpkin Chili with Black Beans

MAKES 6 TO 8 SERVINGS

PREP TIME:
10 minutes

COOK TIME:
45 minutes

I love just about any version of chili that exists. I also love all things fall, including pumpkin treats. It may sound crazy at first to put pumpkin and chili together, but once you taste that combination, you'll be hooked just like I was.

The flavor is subtle, so you almost don't realize the pumpkin is there. What you will notice is a silky texture and lighter feel, which make this chili one of my most unique recipes.

2 tablespoons extra-virgin olive oil

2 cloves garlic, minced

1 yellow onion, diced

1 pound ground beef

2 (15.5-ounce) cans black beans, rinsed and drained

1 (15.5-ounce) can kidney beans, rinsed and drained

1 (15-ounce) can petite diced tomatoes

1 (15-ounce) can unsweetened pumpkin puree

6 tablespoons tomato paste

1 teaspoon chili powder

1 teaspoon ground cumin

½ teaspoon smoked paprika

½ teaspoon onion powder

¼ teaspoon garlic powder

1 teaspoon salt

¼ teaspoon freshly ground black pepper

Tortilla chips, for serving

Shredded Cheddar cheese, for serving

Sliced scallions, for serving

1. In a large pot, heat the oil over medium heat. Add the garlic and onion and cook until the onion is softened, about 5 minutes.

2. Add the ground beef and cook, breaking up the meat with a wooden spoon, until browned, about 7 minutes.

3. Add the beans, diced tomatoes, pumpkin puree, tomato paste, 1 cup water, chili powder, cumin, paprika, onion powder, garlic powder, salt, and pepper. Stir to combine.

4. Bring to a simmer. Cover partially and let simmer, stirring occasionally, about 30 minutes.

5. Serve the chili in bowls with tortilla chips, shredded Cheddar, and sliced scallions.

Eric's Chicken Chili

**MAKES 6 TO
8 SERVINGS**

PREP TIME:
15 minutes

COOK TIME:
35 minutes

This is a dish Eric loves to make because it's light but so filling, and just right for those nights when you need something comforting and nourishing. He pays so much attention to detail and really takes his time to make this chili perfect. Just know that this one can get spicy, so if you're sensitive to heat, you can omit the jalapeño or remove the ribs and seeds for less heat.

2 (15-ounce) cans white beans, rinsed and drained

1 tablespoon extra-virgin olive oil

1 large yellow onion, chopped

1 jalapeño, minced

1 poblano pepper, chopped

4 cloves garlic, minced

Salt and freshly ground black pepper

1 tablespoon ground cumin

1½ teaspoons ground coriander

1 teaspoon ancho chile powder

4 cups low-sodium chicken broth

Juice of 2 limes, plus lime wedges for serving

1 rotisserie chicken, skin removed and meat shredded

¼ cup chopped fresh cilantro, plus more for serving

Tortilla chips, coarsely crushed, for serving

1. Add half the beans to a blender. Pulse two or three times to puree. Set aside until needed.

2. In a large pot, heat the oil over medium-high heat. Add the onion, jalapeño, poblano, and garlic and cook until softened and fragrant, about 5 minutes. Season with salt and pepper to taste. Add the cumin, coriander, and ancho chile powder and cook about 1 minute more to toast the spices. Stir in the chicken broth and lime juice and bring to a simmer, about 5 minutes. Add the whole and pureed beans and continue to simmer until the chili is thickened, about 20 minutes.

3. Taste and adjust the seasonings to your liking. Stir in the rotisserie chicken and cilantro and continue to cook until the chicken is heated through, about 5 minutes more.

4. Ladle the chili into bowls and serve topped with crushed tortilla chips, more chopped cilantro, and a lime wedge.

Okra Soup

**MAKES 4 TO
6 SERVINGS**

PREP TIME:
10 minutes

COOK TIME:
30 minutes

This is soup for those days when you haven't had time to shop but you want to whip up something healthy and filling for lunch or dinner. Almost every ingredient can be kept in your pantry or freezer and brought out at a moment's notice. Then, *bam*! You've got a pot of delicious, hearty soup packed with flavor.

2 tablespoons extra-virgin olive oil

1 red bell pepper, diced

½ white onion, diced

2 cloves garlic, minced

3 slices uncooked bacon, chopped

2 cups sliced fresh or frozen okra

¾ cup fresh or frozen yellow corn

2 (15-ounce) cans white beans, rinsed and drained

4 cups chicken broth

1 teaspoon garlic powder

½ teaspoon dried parsley

Salt and freshly ground black pepper

Cooked white rice, for serving

1. In a large pot or Dutch oven, heat the oil over medium heat. Add the bell pepper, onion, and garlic and cook until softened, about 5 minutes. In a separate pan, fry the bacon until crisp, 3 to 5 minutes. Remove to a plate.

2. To the pot, add in the okra, corn, beans, chicken broth, garlic powder, and dried parsley. Season with salt and pepper. Bring to a low boil, then reduce the heat to medium-low, stir in the cooked bacon, and cover. Let simmer until the beans are tender, 15 to 20 minutes. Serve over white rice.

The Best Chicken Tortilla Soup

MAKES 4 TO 6 SERVINGS

PREP TIME:
10 minutes

COOK TIME:
4 to 6 hours

I know that's a pretty big statement, but I truly believe this is the best chicken tortilla soup recipe I've ever made. When you make soup in a slow cooker, the flavors really intensify, and you get that simmered-all-day feel without having to watch the stove for hours and hours. Then, when the family is ready to eat, you have a big pot of flavorful soup waiting!

2 tablespoons extra-virgin olive oil

1 yellow onion, diced

1 red bell pepper, chopped

3 cloves garlic, finely minced

1 teaspoon garlic powder

¼ teaspoon chili powder

1 cup frozen corn

1 (8-ounce) jar salsa (your favorite kind)

1 (6-ounce) jar enchilada sauce

2 cups shredded rotisserie chicken meat

4 cups chicken broth

Sea salt and freshly ground black pepper

1 cup shredded Mexican cheese blend, plus more for serving

Sour cream, chopped fresh cilantro, sliced avocado, and coarsely crushed tortilla chips, for serving

1. In a Dutch oven or large pot, heat the oil over medium heat. Add the onion and bell pepper and cook until softened, 3 to 4 minutes. Add the minced garlic, garlic powder, and chili powder and cook, stirring constantly, for 30 seconds.

2. Add the sautéed veggies, corn, salsa, enchilada sauce, chicken, and broth to a slow cooker. Season with salt and pepper. Cover and cook on Low for 6 hours or High for 4 hours.

3. When ready to serve, add the shredded cheese to the slow cooker and stir to combine.

4. Ladle into bowls and top with more cheese, sour cream, cilantro, avocado, and tortilla chips.

Good for Ya!

White Beans and Rice

MAKES 4 TO
6 SERVINGS

PREP TIME:
4 hours

COOK TIME:
1 hour 35 minutes

White beans and rice is one of my favorite childhood dishes. It reminds me of my mama in the kitchen making us a whole pot of comforting Louisiana goodness!

1 pound dried cannellini beans

1 bay leaf

2 teaspoons Tony Chachere's Creole Seasoning

Salt and freshly ground black pepper

1 tablespoon extra-virgin olive oil

1 (12-ounce) package fully cooked smoked sausage links, sliced

½ yellow onion, diced

½ green bell pepper, diced

2 cups cooked jasmine rice, for serving

Corn bread, for serving

1. Add the beans to a large container and cover with water. Soak for at least 4 hours or overnight. Rinse and drain.

2. In a large pot, add the soaked beans and enough water to cover them by 2 inches. Add the bay leaf and season with the Tony's seasoning and salt and pepper. Bring to a boil over medium heat, then reduce the heat to medium-low and simmer, stirring frequently and adding more water as needed, until the beans are softened, about 1 hour.

3. Remove the bay leaf and use a potato masher or the back of a large spoon to smash about half the beans. Add more water to the pot if the beans are too thick and continue to simmer.

4. In a large skillet, heat the oil over medium heat. Add the sausage and cook until heated through, 3 to 5 minutes. Add the onion and bell pepper and cook until softened, about 5 minutes. Increase the heat to medium-high and continue cooking until the sausage is nice and browned, about 5 minutes more.

5. Add the sausage mixture to the pot of beans and continue to simmer for 20 minutes, adding more water as needed if the mixture becomes too thick.

6. Serve the white beans and sausage over the rice, with a side of corn bread.

Beef Stew

MAKES 8 SERVINGS

PREP TIME:
15 minutes

COOK TIME:
1 hour 25 minutes

The ultimate winter comfort food has got to be beef stew. It's thick and rich with those big hunks of meat and potatoes that just stick to your ribs and keep you full and happy. This takes a little time to put together, so pull it out on a chilly Sunday afternoon when you can let it simmer.

Make sure to serve it with a batch of warm Southern Buttermilk Biscuits (page 28) and finish it off with a batch of Double-Trouble Chocolate Brownies (page 237)!

3 tablespoons all-purpose flour

1 tablespoon garlic powder

½ teaspoon sea salt

1½ pounds chuck roast, cut into 2-inch cubes

2 tablespoons extra-virgin olive oil

1 tablespoon unsalted butter

3 cups beef broth

3 tablespoons tomato paste

3 large carrots, peeled and sliced into coins

3 stalks celery, chopped

1 yellow onion, coarsely chopped

3 cloves garlic, minced

2 pounds Yukon Gold potatoes, halved

2 cups mushrooms, quartered

2 tablespoons minced fresh parsley, for garnish

1. Add the flour, garlic powder, and sea salt to a large bowl and stir to combine. Toss the beef in the flour mixture until well-coated. Set aside.

2. In a large pot or Dutch oven, heat the oil and butter over medium heat. Add the beef and cook until browned on all sides, stirring frequently, about 5 minutes.

3. Pour the beef broth into the pot and stir with a wooden spoon, scraping up any browned bits stuck to the bottom. Add the tomato paste, carrots, celery, onion, and garlic and stir to combine. Partially cover with a lid and simmer until the meat is tender, about 1 hour.

4. Once the meat is tender, add the potatoes and mushrooms and stir. Cook until the potatoes are fork tender and the stew is thickened, about 20 minutes more. Garnish with the parsley.

Chicken Thigh Bake

MAKES 5 SERVINGS

PREP TIME:
20 minutes

COOK TIME:
1 hour 10 minutes

It doesn't get more comforting than this dish. It's bursting with delicious flavors that fit together so perfectly. This is a newer recipe; I made it for the first time on a cool, crisp fall day, and it was so darn good it became a recurring monthly meal in the Decker house.

Good for Ya!

5 bone-in, skin-on chicken thighs

½ teaspoon garlic powder

½ teaspoon onion powder

Salt and freshly ground black pepper

2 tablespoons extra-virgin olive oil

4 tablespoons (½ stick) unsalted butter

1 yellow onion, diced

4 large cloves garlic, minced

2 cups fresh or frozen cut green beans

3 to 5 Yukon Gold potatoes, cubed

2 cups baby carrots

1 cup chicken broth

1½ cups long-grain white rice

Chopped fresh parsley, for garnish

1. Preheat the oven to 350°F.

2. Season the chicken all over with the garlic powder, onion powder, salt, and pepper. In a large Dutch oven, heat the oil over medium-high heat. Add the chicken and brown on one side for 3 to 5 minutes, then flip and brown on the other side for another 3 to 5 minutes. Transfer to a plate.

3. Reduce the heat to medium and add the butter to the pot to melt. Stir in the diced onion and garlic and cook until the garlic is lightly browned, 3 to 4 minutes. Add the green beans, potatoes, and baby carrots. Pour in ½ cup of the chicken broth, cover, and cook until the potatoes are just tender, 7 to 10 minutes.

4. In a medium pot, combine the rice and 3 cups water and a pinch of salt. Bring to a boil, reduce the heat to low, cover, and cook until the water is absorbed, about 15 minutes.

5. Add the cooked rice to the pot of veggies and stir to combine. Add the chicken and pour in the remaining ½ cup chicken broth. Cover and bake in the oven until the chicken is cooked through and the rice is tender, 15 to 20 minutes Uncover and continue to bake until the chicken skin is nice and crisp, another 5 to 10 minutes.

6. Garnish with parsley and serve.

Skinny Bison Chili

MAKES 6 SERVINGS

PREP TIME:
15 minutes

COOK TIME:
40 minutes

I started making bison chili when we lived in Colorado. I shopped at this little local market, and one day they were out of ground beef. All they had left was ground bison. I asked the gentleman behind the counter what the difference is. He said bison tastes better and is leaner, with less fat and more protein. I decided to give it a go. He was right. I was going to include this recipe in my last book, but I already had too many chili recipes. So I decided to save it for this one.

2 tablespoons extra-virgin olive oil

2 tablespoons minced garlic

½ onion, diced

1 green bell pepper, diced

1 red bell pepper, diced

2 pounds ground bison

2 teaspoons smoked paprika

2 teaspoons dried thyme

1 teaspoon garlic powder

½ teaspoon chili powder

1 (10-ounce) can diced tomatoes with green chilis

1 (6-ounce) can tomato paste

1 tablespoon Worcestershire sauce

2 teaspoons ground cinnamon

Pinch of sea salt and freshly ground black pepper

Cooked brown rice or cauliflower rice, chopped fresh cilantro, and sliced jalapeño (optional), for serving

1. In a large pot or Dutch oven, heat the oil over medium heat. Add the garlic, onion, and bell peppers and cook until the onion begins to brown, about 8 minutes.

2. Add the ground bison, along with the paprika, thyme, garlic powder, and chili powder. Cook, breaking up the meat with a wooden spoon, until browned and cooked through, 6 to 8 minutes. Stir in 1 cup water, the diced tomatoes, and the tomato paste. Add the Worcestershire, cinnamon, salt, and pepper.

3. Reduce the heat to medium-low, cover, and cook until the chili has thickened and the beans are tender, about 25 minutes.

4. Serve the chili over brown rice or, for fewer carbs, cauliflower rice. Top with chopped cilantro and sliced jalapeño, if desired.

5

I have a handful of true loves in my life: my family, my friends, my music, the beach—and pasta!

OK, so the pasta part might have been a little dramatic, but if you know me, you know how much I love food, especially pasta. Everything just seems right in the world when I've got a big plate of spaghetti in front of me and I dig in with a fork in one hand, twirling the noodles, and a glass of red wine in the other. I don't know if it's in my blood or if it's environmental, but I love everything about pasta and coming up with new and unique ways to enjoy every bite.

Pasta Lover

One-Pot Ground Turkey Spinach Rigatoni

**MAKES 4 TO
6 SERVINGS**

PREP TIME:
10 minutes

COOK TIME:
40 minutes

Sometimes you just need to cook an easy, crowd-pleasing meal that even the picky eaters will love. This one is always a hit. It's a flavorful, delicious dish that will warm everyone up on those days when the air is crisp and you're ready to turn on the fireplace. Serve this as is from the stovetop, or throw it in a casserole dish, top it with cheese, and bake it.

5 slices thick-cut applewood or maple bacon, chopped

2 tablespoons extra-virgin olive oil

1/2 medium yellow onion, diced

3 cloves garlic, minced

1 pound ground turkey

1 teaspoon garlic powder

1 teaspoon salt

1/4 teaspoon freshly ground black pepper

4 cups chicken broth

1 (6-ounce) can tomato paste

10 ounces rigatoni

1/2 cup half-and-half

1/2 cup grated Parmesan cheese, plus more for serving

1/2 cup shredded mozzarella cheese

3 cups baby spinach

1. Add the bacon to a large Dutch oven or pot over medium-high heat. Cook until lightly crisped, 5 to 7 minutes. Transfer to a plate lined with paper towels and discard the extra grease from the pot.

2. In the same pot, heat the oil over medium heat. Add the onion and cook until translucent, 5 to 7 minutes. Add the garlic and cook until just fragrant, 1 to 2 minutes.

3. Add the ground turkey, garlic powder, salt, and pepper and cook, breaking up the meat with a wooden spoon, until cooked through, 6 to 8 minutes.

4. Add the chicken broth, tomato paste, and pasta, increase the heat to high, and bring to a boil. Reduce the heat to medium, partially cover, and cook, stirring occasionally, until the pasta is al dente, about 10 minutes.

5. Add the half-and-half and cook until the sauce thickens, about 5 minutes. Fold in the Parmesan and mozzarella, then the spinach, one cup at a time, until wilted.

6. Serve the rigatoni topped with more Parmesan.

Easy Sausage and Pepper Pasta

MAKES 4 TO 6 SERVINGS

PREP TIME:
10 minutes

COOK TIME:
15 minutes

There are certain dishes that come together when I'm playing *Chopped* at home and I'm in a time crunch. I walk to my pantry, I look in the fridge, and I think, *What can I throw together that's delicious and quick with just these ingredients I found since I didn't pre-plan?* That's how this one came to be. I had a few sausage links, bell peppers from the garden, some onion—and *boom*! The family loved this simple dish so much that it became part of the dinner rotation. It's hearty, savory, filling, and it can feed lots of mouths, which makes me happy.

You can use andouille sausage or your favorite sausage. I like the turkey, pork, and beef combo, and I like it mild so the kids can handle the heat. Use all one color of bell pepper if you prefer. I happen to like the different colors and the hint of different flavors among the three. You can sprinkle the finished dish with Parmesan or leave it as is. The kids like it with cheese, but I prefer it without!

3 tablespoons extra-virgin olive oil

3 links fully cooked mild or spicy sausage, sliced

1 small yellow onion, thinly sliced

1 red bell pepper, thinly sliced

½ green bell pepper, thinly sliced

½ yellow bell pepper, thinly sliced

2 cloves garlic, minced

Salt

10 ounces spaghetti

1 teaspoon garlic powder

Freshly ground black pepper

Grated Parmesan cheese, for garnish (optional)

1. In a large skillet, heat 1 tablespoon oil over medium heat. Add the sausage and cook, turning frequently, until lightly browned, about 5 minutes. Add the onion and bell peppers and cook, stirring, until the vegetables are softened, 5 to 8 minutes. Add the garlic and cook, stirring, until fragrant, about 1 minute. Cover and remove from the heat.

2. Meanwhile, in a large pot of salted boiling water, cook the spaghetti to al dente according to the package directions.

3. Drain the pasta and add to the skillet with the sausage mixture. Drizzle with the remaining 2 tablespoons oil and season with the garlic powder and salt and pepper. Toss well to coat. Serve with grated Parmesan if desired.

Mussels Linguine

MAKES 6 SERVINGS

PREP TIME:
25 minutes

COOK TIME:
25 minutes

Everyone knows my love for pasta, but my love for seafood is almost as strong. I grew up eating mostly shrimp, crab, and lobster, and I didn't get introduced to the other parts of the sea until I was older. When I had mussels and pasta at a hole-in-the-wall Italian spot, I was hooked. I immediately went home and was on a mission to re-create this incredible dish that was love at first bite.

6 tablespoons unsalted butter, plus more if needed

1 tablespoon extra-virgin olive oil, plus more if needed

3 shallots, sliced

5 cloves garlic, minced

Salt and freshly ground black pepper

Crushed red pepper flakes (if you like it spicy)

1 teaspoon garlic powder

2 cups white wine, plus more if needed

12 to 16 fresh mussels, cleaned and debearded (see note)

1 pound linguine

3 tablespoons chopped fresh parsley, plus more for serving

Juice of 1 lemon, plus lemon wedges (optional) for serving

1. In a large skillet, heat 3 tablespoons butter and the oil over medium-high heat until the butter is melted. Add the shallots and garlic and cook until softened and fragrant, about 5 minutes. Season with salt, pepper, and pepper flakes to taste and the garlic powder. Add the wine and bring to a boil until reduced by half, about 5 minutes.

2. Add the mussels to the skillet and reduce the heat to medium. Cover with a tight-fitting lid and cook until all the shells have popped open, 5 to 7 minutes. Toss away any mussels that don't open (it means they're no good). At this point, taste the sauce and add a splash more wine and/or more butter or oil if needed. Reduce the heat to low and let simmer while you make the pasta.

3. Meanwhile, in a large pot of salted boiling water, cook the pasta to al dente according to the package directions.

4. Drain the pasta and transfer to a bowl. Add the remaining 3 tablespoons butter, the parsley, and lemon juice and toss until coated. Season with salt and pepper.

5. Add the pasta to the skillet with the mussels and toss to coat. Garnish with more parsley and serve with lemon wedges (if you wanna get real fancy).

Jessie's note:

They can have a decent amount of grit and dirt on them if they are fresh. Clean them thoroughly by rinsing and gently scrubbing the outsides. To debeard the mussels, just find the brown fibrous piece around the seam of the shell and gently pull to remove.

American Spaghetti

MAKES 6 TO 8 SERVINGS

PREP TIME:
5 minutes

COOK TIME:
45 minutes

My mom made this spaghetti for us weekly when I was growing up, and now I make it for my family. It's one of those comfort meals that I love to have when I come back from a big trip. It just feels and tastes like home. We call it American spaghetti because, well, there is nothing Italian about it. (I am part Italian, so I have to make sure to reiterate that I know this is very Americanized.) It doesn't matter, though, because I still love it! It's a great go-to for the family and super easy to make. I guarantee this will become a regular meal for your family too.

2 tablespoons extra-virgin olive oil

½ white onion, diced

4 cloves garlic, minced

2 pounds lean ground beef

1 (29-ounce) can tomato sauce

1 (10-ounce) can Ro*tel diced tomatoes

1 (8-ounce) can mushrooms, drained

2 teaspoons dried basil

1 teaspoon garlic powder

1 teaspoon Italian seasoning

½ teaspoon sugar

½ teaspoon onion powder

¼ teaspoon salt

¼ teaspoon freshly ground black pepper

1 pound spaghetti

Garlic bread, for serving

1. In a large skillet, heat the oil over medium-low heat. Add the diced onion and cook until softened, about 10 minutes. Add the garlic and continue to cook for about 1 minute.

2. Increase the heat to medium-high and add the ground beef. Cook, breaking up the meat with a wooden spoon, until browned, 10 to 12 minutes.

3. Add the tomato sauce, diced tomatoes, and mushrooms and stir to combine.

4. Add the basil, garlic powder, Italian seasoning, sugar, onion powder, salt, and pepper. Taste and adjust the seasonings to your liking. Cover, reduce the heat to medium, and let simmer for about 20 minutes.

5. Meanwhile, in a large pot of salted boiling water, cook the spaghetti to al dente according to the package directions.

6. Drain the pasta and add to the skillet with the meat sauce. Toss to combine and serve with warm garlic bread.

Easy Family-Style Chicken and Broccoli Pasta

MAKES 4 TO 6 SERVINGS

PREP TIME:
10 minutes

COOK TIME:
30 minutes

When I was a little girl, there was a bag of broccoli pasta from the grocery store that my mama would make for a fast meal, and I remember it being so delicious. Now, my mama made pretty much everything from scratch and if she didn't, she doctored it up to make it even better. I can't recall the exact recipe. This is as close to it as I can get from my little-girl memory, and my family now loves it too!

10 ounces farfalle pasta

8 slices bacon, chopped

2 tablespoons extra-virgin olive oil

1/2 cup diced yellow onion

4 cloves garlic, minced

1 (10-ounce) bag frozen broccoli, thawed

2 (12.5-ounce) cans chunk chicken breast, drained

1 teaspoon garlic powder

1/4 teaspoon sea salt

1/4 teaspoon freshly ground black pepper

1 cup unsweetened almond milk, plus more if needed

1 cup shredded Parmesan cheese

1 cup shredded mozzarella cheese

Sliced French bread and butter, for serving

1. In a large pot of salted boiling water, cook the pasta to al dente according to the package directions. Drain.

2. Meanwhile, in a large skillet or Dutch oven over medium-high heat, cook the bacon, stirring occasionally, until browned, about 5 minutes. Transfer the bacon to a plate lined with paper towels and wipe out most of the grease from the pan.

3. In the same pan, heat the oil over medium heat. Add the diced onion and garlic and cook until the onion is translucent, about 5 minutes.

4. Add the broccoli and chicken, then add the garlic powder, salt, and pepper. Cook, stirring, until heated through, about 5 minutes.

5. Increase the heat to medium-high, add the almond milk and both cheeses, and stir to combine. Cook until the cheese is melted and the sauce has thickened, 5 to 7 minutes. Add the drained pasta and cook for 5 minutes more, adding more milk if the sauce gets too thick.

6. Portion the pasta into bowls and serve with French bread and butter.

Mushroom Ravioli

MAKES 4 SERVINGS

PREP TIME:
5 minutes

COOK TIME:
15 minutes

I made this tasty dish for Christmas one year and the family went crazy over it. It's so flavorful and fragrant with every bite, you'll want to lick the plate clean. It's not technically a Christmas recipe, so serve this with warm bread and Destin Dipping Oil (page 38) any time of year.

1 pound cheese ravioli

2 tablespoons extra-virgin olive oil

1 shallot, thinly sliced

2 ounces diced pancetta

10 ounces mixed mushrooms, sliced

Sea salt and freshly ground black pepper

4 tablespoons (½ stick) unsalted butter

2 cloves garlic, minced

2 tablespoons fresh thyme leaves

1 tablespoon chopped fresh sage

3 tablespoons balsamic vinegar

¼ cup heavy cream

Pinch of crushed red pepper flakes

Grated Parmesan cheese, for serving

1. In a large pot of salted boiling water, cook the ravioli according to the package directions. Drain.

2. Meanwhile, in a large skillet, heat the oil over medium-high heat. Add the shallot and sauté until soft, 2 to 3 minutes. Add the pancetta and fry to crisp, 2 to 3 minutes. Add the mushrooms to the pan and cook, stirring occasionally, until the mushrooms deepen in color and release their liquid, 3 to 5 minutes. Season with salt and pepper.

3. Add the butter, garlic, thyme, and sage and sauté until the garlic is fragrant, 1 to 2 minutes. Add the balsamic vinegar and heavy cream and continue to cook for 5 minutes, then add the ravioli and toss to coat. Serve topped with the pepper flakes and grated Parmesan.

Ground Beef Lasagna

MAKES 10 TO 12 SERVINGS

PREP TIME: 20 minutes

COOK TIME: 1 hour

I pride myself on making some of the best lasagna out there, which is why it's on the cover of my book! The ricotta cheese spread perfectly on the layers, the delicious ground beef marinara sauce, the extra hunks of Parmesan cheese—this lasagna will become a family and friends favorite.

1 pound lasagna noodles

3 tablespoons extra-virgin olive oil

1 yellow onion, diced

1 cup diced carrots

4 cloves garlic, minced

1 pound lean ground beef

2 tablespoons tomato paste

Sea salt and freshly ground black pepper

1 (24-ounce) jar marinara sauce

1 (16-ounce) container ricotta cheese

1 (8-ounce) block Parmesan cheese, cut into ½-inch cubes (see note)

6 cups shredded mozzarella cheese

Fresh basil leaves, for garnish

1. In a large pot of salted boiling water, cook the lasagna noodles according to the package directions. Drain and spread out on a baking sheet.

2. Meanwhile, in a large skillet, heat 2 tablespoons oil over medium heat. Add the onion and carrots and cook until tender, about 5 minutes. Add the garlic and cook until fragrant, about 2 minutes. Add the ground beef and tomato paste, season with salt and pepper, and continue to cook, breaking up the meat with a wooden spoon, until the meat begins to brown, 8 to 10 minutes. Remove from the heat.

3. Preheat the oven to 400°F and grease a 9 x 13-inch baking dish with the remaining 1 tablespoon oil.

4. Layer the bottom of the dish with one-third of the lasagna noodles. Top with one-third of the beef mixture, a ladle of the marinara sauce, and one-third of the ricotta cheese. Dot the ricotta with one-third of the Parmesan cubes, followed by one-quarter of the mozzarella. Repeat this layering two more times, then finish with a layer of marinara and the remaining mozzarella.

5. Transfer the lasagna to the oven and bake for 30 to 40 minutes. The lasagna is ready when a toothpick sinks into the center, showing that the noodles are tender. Let cool for 15 to 20 minutes before garnishing with basil and serving.

Jessie's note:

My secret to the most amazing lasagna of your life is all in the little Parmesan cheese bombs. I use a good size block of cheese and cut it into cubes to dot on the layer of ricotta. What you get are these big surprise bites of cheesy goodness in every square.

Chicken, Spinach, and Pasta Bake

MAKES 4 TO 6 SERVINGS

PREP TIME:
15 minutes

COOK TIME:
30 minutes

I love a good casserole, and let me tell you, *this* one will be a go-to dinner in your home too. It's easy and quick, and it will fill up everyone's belly in no time. I love the creamy, cheesy bites—not to mention the addition of the sneaky spinach. You will want to serve this with some yummy bread, so you can soak up all the creamy goodness on your plate.

8 ounces penne

3 cups half-and-half

2 tablespoons all-purpose flour

1 teaspoon dried basil

1 teaspoon dried oregano

1 teaspoon Tony Chachere's Creole Seasoning

½ teaspoon Italian seasoning

Sea salt and freshly ground black pepper

2 tablespoons unsalted butter

½ cup diced onion

2 cloves garlic, minced

2 cups grated Parmesan cheese

2 cups shredded mozzarella cheese

1 rotisserie chicken, meat shredded

½ cup chicken broth

1 (6-ounce) bag fresh spinach

1. Preheat the oven to 400°F.

2. In a large pot of salted boiling water, cook the pasta to al dente according to the package directions. Drain.

3. In a small bowl, whisk together the half-and-half, flour, basil, oregano, Tony's seasoning, and Italian seasoning until combined. Season with salt and pepper.

4. In a large pot, melt the butter over medium-high heat. Add the onion and garlic and cook until the garlic is fragrant, about 3 minutes.

5. Add the half-and-half mixture, reduce the heat to medium, and cook, stirring occasionally, until slightly thickened, about 5 minutes. Stir in the Parmesan and 1 cup mozzarella.

6. Add the shredded chicken and chicken broth to the pot and let simmer for about 5 minutes. Turn off the heat and season with salt and pepper. Add the spinach and pasta. Gently fold everything together until the spinach is wilted, then pour into a 9 x 13-inch baking dish or 3½-quart Dutch oven. Top with the remaining 1 cup mozzarella and bake, uncovered, until hot and bubbling, about 15 minutes.

6

Everyone needs a good sidekick for their meal! The perfect side can really enhance and bring out the flavors of the main course—but more than that, nothing says comfort like some good sides. These are some of my favorite side dishes that I handpicked to pair with the main courses in this book, from crispy honey Brussels sprouts to serve alongside your meat to perfectly fried hush puppies to lap up your soup.

Pick Your Sidekick

Oven-Roasted Honey Brussels Sprouts

MAKES 4 TO 6 SERVINGS

PREP TIME:
5 minutes

COOK TIME:
35 minutes

It's as easy as one, two, three, steps—that's all it takes to whip up the perfect side for any meal. I like to use fresh Brussels sprouts, but you can use frozen if needed to throw together this delicious green side at the last minute.

1½ pounds Brussels sprouts, trimmed and halved

2 tablespoons extra-virgin olive oil

¼ teaspoon garlic powder

Sea salt and freshly ground black pepper

2 tablespoons balsamic vinegar

1 tablespoon honey

1. Preheat the oven to 400°F and line a baking sheet with foil or parchment paper.

2. Toss the Brussels sprouts on the prepared baking sheet with the oil, garlic powder, and salt and pepper. Roast until tender and lightly browned, tossing halfway through, 30 to 35 minutes.

3. In a large serving bowl, whisk together the vinegar and honey. Add the roasted Brussels sprouts and toss to coat completely before serving.

Toasted Almond Rice

MAKES 6 SERVINGS

PREP TIME:
5 minutes

COOK TIME:
55 minutes

I discovered almond rice at one of my favorite restaurants and instantly fell in love with it. The flavors of coconut and almond were so unique. I just knew I wanted to have it again and again, so I went home and started experimenting. It's the perfect "side piece" for any dish.

½ cup sliced almonds

1 tablespoon extra-virgin olive oil

½ medium yellow onion, finely diced

1 tablespoon minced garlic

2 cups basmati rice

3 cups chicken broth

1½ cups full-fat or light coconut milk

6 tablespoons unsalted butter

1 teaspoon garlic powder

1 teaspoon sea salt

½ teaspoon freshly ground black pepper

1. Preheat the oven to 375°F.

2. Spread the almonds on a baking sheet in an even layer. Bake until lightly browned, about 5 minutes. Remove from the oven and reduce the heat to 350°F.

3. In an ovenproof large pot, heat the oil over medium heat. Add the onion and garlic and cook until the onion is translucent, 3 to 5 minutes.

4. Add the rice and cook for a few minutes more, stirring to coat completely in the oil.

5. Add the chicken broth and coconut milk and increase the heat to medium-high. Bring to a gentle boil, then remove from the heat and cover with a lid or foil. Transfer to the oven and bake until the rice is tender and easily fluffed with a fork, 40 to 50 minutes.

6. Reserve about 2 tablespoons of the toasted almonds for garnishing and fold the rest into the rice. Slice the butter into 1-inch pats and stir into the rice. Season with the garlic powder, salt, and pepper and toss to fluff the rice. Transfer to a large serving dish and garnish with the reserved toasted almonds.

Succotash

MAKES 6 SERVINGS

PREP TIME:
15 minutes

COOK TIME:
25 minutes

If you're not from the South or you've never had succotash, y'all are missing out. The flavors are so fresh and delicious, making it the perfect side for just about any meal. Depending on who you talk to, succotash can be made with all seasonal veggies, lima beans or butter beans, tomatoes, you name it. For this recipe, I like using butter beans and keeping the veggies simple but without missing any of the flavor.

4 slices center-cut bacon, roughly chopped

3 tablespoons unsalted butter

½ cup chopped yellow onion

½ cup diced red bell pepper

½ cup diced green bell pepper

2 cloves garlic, minced

1 teaspoon dried oregano

1 teaspoon paprika

½ teaspoon garlic powder

1 (15-ounce) can butter beans

3 cups fresh or frozen white kernel corn

1 cup sliced fresh or frozen okra

Sea salt and freshly ground black pepper

1. In a large skillet or nonstick frying pan over medium-high heat, cook the bacon until just starting to crisp, about 5 minutes. Transfer to a plate lined with paper towels and wipe out the skillet.

2. In the same skillet, melt the butter over medium heat. Add the onion and bell peppers and cook until tender, 5 to 8 minutes. Add the minced garlic, oregano, paprika, and garlic powder and cook until fragrant, about 1 minute.

3. Add the beans, corn, okra, and bacon and stir to combine. Reduce the heat to low, cover, and cook until heated through, 5 to 8 minutes.

Hush Puppies

MAKES ABOUT 2 DOZEN HUSH PUPPIES

PREP TIME:
10 minutes

COOK TIME:
15 minutes

A fish dinner just isn't complete without a side of steaming-hot freshly fried hush puppies. Now you can buy a mix where all you have to do is add water, but with just a handful of ingredients you can make these from scratch and they are ten times better! The key is to make sure your batter is just right, not too dry and not too wet.

Peanut or canola oil, for frying

1 cup yellow cornmeal

⅓ cup all-purpose flour

2 tablespoons sugar

1 teaspoon baking powder

¼ teaspoon baking soda

½ teaspoon salt

1 large egg, lightly beaten

½ cup buttermilk

1 small yellow onion, finely chopped

Honey butter, for serving

1. Fill a large Dutch oven or deep pot with enough oil to cover by 3 inches. Heat over medium-high heat until the oil temperature reaches 350°F.

2. Meanwhile, in a large bowl, whisk together the cornmeal, flour, sugar, baking powder, baking soda, and salt. Add the beaten egg and buttermilk and stir to combine. The batter should be moist but not runny. Fold in the onion.

3. Working in batches, drop tablespoonfuls of the batter into the hot oil and fry until golden, turning once, 3 to 5 minutes.

4. Transfer the fried hush puppies to a paper towel–lined plate to cool slightly. Serve with honey butter.

Spiced Skillet Potatoes

MAKES 2 TO
4 SERVINGS

PREP TIME:
10 minutes

COOK TIME:
20 minutes

These curry-seasoned potatoes are Eric's favorite. I will make a roast chicken and have these as a side along with a yummy salad. Eric is a meat-and-potatoes guy, so I'm always coming up with different ways to cook his potatoes. These curry taters just hit the spot for my sweet man. Enjoy!

2 pounds Yukon Gold potatoes, cut into 1½-inch cubes

½ cup extra-virgin olive oil

1 tablespoon yellow curry powder

2 teaspoons garlic powder

1 teaspoon paprika

½ teaspoon fine sea salt

1 tablespoon chopped fresh parsley, for serving

Coarse sea salt, for serving

1. In a large bowl, toss the potatoes with ¼ cup oil, the curry powder, garlic powder, paprika, and fine sea salt.

2. In a large skillet, heat the remaining ¼ cup oil over medium heat. Add the potatoes in an even layer. (You may need to work in batches.) Cover and cook, turning occasionally, until golden brown on all sides and fork tender, about 20 minutes.

3. Serve hot, topped with the parsley and coarse sea salt.

Mexican Street Corn

**MAKES 4 TO
6 SERVINGS**

PREP TIME:
5 minutes

COOK TIME:
15 minutes

If Mexican street corn is on a menu, I can promise you I'm ordering it. It just feels like summer every time I sink my teeth in and get the burst of juices from the corn and the cheese all in one bite.

This recipe is how I make it at home with fresh summer corn, but if you like your corn more tender, you can wrap the ears in foil and grill for 20 minutes. After that, remove the foil and grill for 3 to 5 minutes on each side.

6 ears corn, shucked and cleaned

½ cup mayonnaise

Chili-lime powder (I like the stuff from Trader Joe's)

Sea salt and freshly ground black pepper

⅓ cup grated cotija cheese

¼ cup chopped fresh cilantro

Lime, quartered

1. Preheat a grill or grill pan to medium-high.

2. Arrange the corn directly on the grill or grill pan and cook, turning often, until slightly charred on all sides, 12 to 15 minutes.

3. Brush the corn with the mayonnaise and sprinkle with chili-lime powder, salt and pepper, the cotija cheese, and chopped cilantro. Finish with a squeeze of lime juice and serve.

7

Now, I have a confession to make: I never felt like I put enough pizza recipes in my last cookbook—and that's a crying shame! I love making homemade pizza just as much as I love making a pot of chili or gumbo, but we had simply run out of pages. This time I made sure to add in a handful of my absolute favorites.

When we make pizza at the house, it's always a party. We all gather around as I knead out the dough, spread on the pizza sauce, and add all the toppings. Everyone chimes in on what they want specifically on their pizza. It's always so much fun.

Pizza Party Part II

Mexican Pizza

MAKES 8 SERVINGS

PREP TIME:
10 minutes

COOK TIME:
30 minutes

OK, before you scratch your pretty head and go, *What?*—hear me out. I was at my Kittenish office a couple years ago, and there was this pizza food truck that would sit out front from time to time. Whenever I saw that truck, I would always get excited and go order a pizza and a coke for lunch. One day the chalkboard read, "Mexican taco pizza," and if you know me when it comes to food, then you know I will try anything once. So I ordered it, licked my fingers clean, and now I'm sharing it with you.

Flour, for the work surface

1 pound refrigerated pizza dough, at room temperature (I use Publix brand)

FOR THE TACO MEAT

2 tablespoons extra-virgin olive oil

½ cup diced yellow onion

1 pound ground beef

½ cup tomato sauce

1 tablespoon chili powder

1 teaspoon ground cumin

¼ teaspoon onion powder

¼ teaspoon garlic powder

½ teaspoon salt

¼ teaspoon freshly ground black pepper

FOR THE PIZZA AND TOPPINGS

¾ cup refried beans

2 cups shredded Mexican cheese blend

1 cup shredded lettuce

1 cup diced tomatoes

¼ cup taco sauce

½ cup sliced black olives

½ cup sour cream, for serving

Crushed tortilla chips

1. Preheat the oven to 400°F and dust a work surface with flour. With floured hands, work the pizza dough to your desired thickness and press into a pizza pan or baking sheet. Bake just until the crust begins to firm up, 5 to 10 minutes.

2. Meanwhile, make the taco meat: In a large skillet, heat the oil over medium heat. Add the onion and cook until softened, 3 to 5 minutes. Add the ground beef and cook, breaking up the meat with a wooden spoon, until browned, about 7 minutes. Add the tomato sauce, chili powder, cumin, onion powder, garlic powder, salt, and pepper and stir to combine. Reduce the heat to medium-low and cook for 5 minutes.

3. Remove the pizza crust from the oven and top with the refried beans in an even layer. Spoon on the taco meat and sprinkle with 1 cup cheese. Return to the oven and bake until the crust is browned and the cheese is melted, 5 to 7 minutes.

4. Top the finished pizza with the shredded lettuce, tomatoes, taco sauce, olives, sour cream, remaining 1 cup cheese, and crushed tortilla chips. Slice and serve.

Potato Pizza

MAKES 8 SERVINGS

PREP TIME:
10 minutes

COOK TIME:
25 minutes

When I was growing up in Georgia, there was a famous pizza chain we would go to after soccer games or practice. It was so delicious, and we were always excited to go as a family! My parents would get potato pizza every time. I was always a simple pepperoni girl, but I would beg for a slice of the potato pizza because it was so tasty and different and unique. I've gone back to get that pizza, and it's just not quite the same as my memory of it. I've never seen the original recipe anywhere, so this is how I always make it at home.

Flour, for the work surface

1 pound refrigerated pizza dough, at room temperature (I use Publix brand)

2½ cups cubed baked potato (from about 1 large potato)

3 tablespoons extra-virgin olive oil

2 tablespoons dry ranch seasoning mix

6 slices provolone cheese

10 slices chopped cooked bacon

1 cup shredded mild Cheddar cheese

3 tablespoons sliced scallions

Sour cream, for serving

1. Preheat the oven to 400°F and dust a work surface with flour. With floured hands, work the pizza dough to your desired thickness and press into a pizza pan or baking sheet. Bake just until the crust begins to firm up, 5 to 10 minutes.

2. Meanwhile, in a medium bowl, stir together the potato, oil, and ranch seasoning mix.

3. Remove the pizza crust from the oven and arrange the provolone slices on top. Spoon the potato mixture evenly over the provolone. Sprinkle with the bacon and Cheddar. Return to the oven and bake until the crust is browned and the cheese is melted, 13 to 16 minutes. Sprinkle with the scallions and dollop with sour cream to serve.

Pesto Pizza

MAKES 8 SERVINGS

PREP TIME:
30 minutes

COOK TIME:
25 minutes

Homemade pizzas are always a party, whether it's just the kids and Eric or we're inviting a group of people over and I'm whipping them up left and right for a bit of variety. People will call out the kind of pizzas they want, and I will try to figure it out in the moment. Sometimes the results are magic, and sometimes the amount of laughter is way better than the actual pizza. One night, one of my best friends, who happens to be a pescatarian, was over. He didn't want pepperoni or any other sort of meat on his pizza, so he specifically requested a pesto-mushroom topping. This is what I came up with on the fly, and it was one of those times when the pizza came out beautifully!

Flour, for the work surface

1 pound refrigerated pizza dough, at room temperature (I use Publix brand)

½ cup jarred pesto, plus more for serving

1½ cups grated mozzarella cheese

1 small red onion, thinly sliced

6 white button mushrooms, thinly sliced

½ cup cherry tomatoes, halved

1. Preheat the oven to 400°F and dust a work surface with flour. With floured hands, work the pizza dough to your desired thickness and press into a pizza pan or baking sheet. Bake just until the crust begins to firm up, 5 to 10 minutes.

2. Remove the pizza crust from the oven and brush evenly with the pesto. Top evenly with the mozzarella, onion, mushrooms, and tomatoes. Return to the oven and bake until the crust is browned and the cheese is melted, 10 to 15 minutes. Top with more pesto to serve.

Meat Lover's Pizza

MAKES 8 SERVINGS

PREP TIME:
30 minutes

COOK TIME:
30 minutes

This one might be my favorite of all time because it's got *alllll* the meats! But a meat lover's pizza still needs a little flavor and texture boost, which is why I love to add red onion and sliced bell pepper. Just thinking about this pizza gets my mouth watering, so I know y'all are gonna love it.

Flour, for the work surface

1 pound refrigerated pizza dough, at room temperature (I use Publix brand)

1 tablespoon extra-virgin olive oil

¼ teaspoon garlic powder

½ to ¾ cup pizza sauce

2 cups shredded mozzarella cheese

20 to 30 slices pepperoni

1 cup cooked sausage crumbles

4 ounces Canadian bacon, cut into 1-inch squares

½ cup sliced mushrooms

¼ small red onion, thinly sliced

¼ green bell pepper, sliced

Crushed red pepper flakes, for serving (optional)

1. Preheat the oven to 400°F and dust a work surface with flour. With floured hands, work the pizza dough to your desired thickness and press into a pizza pan or baking sheet. Bake just until the crust begins to firm up, 5 to 10 minutes.

2. Remove the pizza crust from the oven, brush with the oil and sprinkle with the garlic powder. Spread the pizza sauce evenly over the crust, going about 1 inch from the edge. Top with the mozzarella, pepperoni, sausage, Canadian bacon, mushrooms, onion, and bell pepper. Return to the oven and bake until the crust is browned and the cheese is melted, 10 to 15 minutes. Serve topped with pepper flakes if ya like it spicy.

8

In my first cookbook, I had a whole chapter dedicated to my love of meat, and this one is no exception. Here is another handful of my favorite dishes that center around my love of meat! Whether it's a classic ground beef meatloaf or a crispy fried chicken sandwich, there's something to satisfy all your meaty cravings.

Poultry & Beef

Recipes with ○ icon indicate "Good for Ya!" recipes.

Meatloaf

MAKES 6 SERVINGS

PREP TIME:
15 minutes

COOK TIME:
1 hour 10 minutes

Meatloaf is one of those things that people either love or hate. I think that's because they haven't tried my meatloaf—ha! Nothing beats a big slice of moist and juicy meatloaf with that sweet, caramelized glaze of tomato sauce on top! If you've never had a good one, you have to give my tried-and-true recipe a shot.

3 large eggs, beaten

1/2 cup whole milk

1 green bell pepper, finely diced

1/2 white onion, finely diced

1 teaspoon sea salt

1/4 teaspoon freshly ground black pepper

2 pounds lean ground beef

3/4 cup panko bread crumbs

1 teaspoon garlic powder

1/2 teaspoon Tony Chachere's Creole Seasoning

1/2 teaspoon paprika

1/2 teaspoon dried parsley

3 fresh mint leaves, chopped

2 teaspoons Worcestershire sauce

TOPPING

1/2 cup ketchup

2 tablespoons brown sugar

1 teaspoon yellow mustard

1. Preheat the oven to 350°F and line a baking sheet with foil or parchment paper.

2. In a large bowl, stir together the beaten eggs, bell pepper, onion, salt, and pepper.

3. To a separate large bowl, add the beef, panko, garlic powder, Tony's seasoning, paprika, parsley, and mint. With clean hands, mix together until well combined.

4. Place the meat mixture on the prepared baking sheet and form into a loaf. (It doesn't need to look perfect!) Bake for 30 minutes.

5. Meanwhile, make the topping: In a small bowl, stir together the ketchup, brown sugar, and yellow mustard.

6. After the meatloaf has baked for 30 minutes, remove from the oven and spread all over with the ketchup mixture. Return to the oven and bake until the meatloaf reaches an internal temperature of 160°F, 30 to 40 minutes.

7. Let the meatloaf rest for 15 minutes before slicing to serve.

Slow Cooker Pulled Pork Sammiches

MAKES 8 TO
10 SERVINGS

PREP TIME:
15 minutes

COOK TIME:
12 hours

If we're entertaining and want to make a quick and easy main dish to serve a lot of people, it's got to be pulled pork sammiches. My favorite recipes are the ones you can just throw together and let the slow cooker do all the work. You know it's gonna be easy, and you know it's gonna be good!

I like to mix a little barbecue sauce into the meat to keep it moist, but I also serve sauce on the side so people can fix the sandwiches to their liking. And don't forget the pickle chips and slaw!

1 pork shoulder or pork butt (6 to 7 pounds bone-in, or 5 to 6 pounds boneless), trimmed

2 tablespoons salt

1 teaspoon freshly ground black pepper

1 tablespoon garlic powder

1 tablespoon brown sugar

2 teaspoons Worcestershire sauce

4 cloves garlic, crushed

1 red onion, cut into 1-inch wedges

½ cup barbecue sauce, plus more for serving (see note)

TO SERVE

8 to 10 Hawaiian rolls, split

Dill pickle chips and store-bought or homemade coleslaw

1. Pat the pork dry with paper towels. Season all over with the salt, pepper, and garlic powder, then rub all over with the brown sugar. Place the pork in a 6-quart or larger slow cooker and pour in ½ cup water and the Worcestershire. Scatter the garlic and onion around the pork.

2. Cover and cook on Low until the meat is tender and falling apart, 10 to 12 hours. Carefully transfer the meat to a large cutting board and use two forks to shred the meat into small pieces. Remove the bone and any large hunks of fat. You can reserve some of the cooking liquid to add to leftovers if you'd like, or just toss it.

3. Transfer the shredded meat back to the slow cooker and mix in the barbecue sauce; toss to coat. Cover and keep on Warm until ready to serve. To serve, add a scoop of pulled pork on a Hawaiian roll and top with dill pickle chips, coleslaw, and more barbecue sauce.

Jessie's note:

I love using Trader Joe's Organic Sriracha Roasted Garlic BBQ Sauce for a little extra kick!

Oven-Roasted Beef Tenderloin

MAKES 8 SERVINGS

PREP TIME:
15 minutes

COOK TIME:
1 hour 15 minutes

When I say this is a tenderloin, I mean that loin is gonna be *tender*. And because it's such a beautiful cut of meat, it isn't difficult to get the juiciest and most flavorful loin roasted right in the oven. Just remember to go low and slow. Trust me, if you serve this, your dinner guests are in for an amazing meal, and you'll hear the compliments all night long. A 4-pound tenderloin will feed a good number of people with leftovers, but it can be pricey. If you're looking for a smaller portion, just ask at the butcher counter, and they will cut the size you need and usually tie up the meat for you. Pair this with my simply perfect Mashed Potatoes and green beans and enjoy!

Cooking spray, for the baking sheet

1 (4-pound) beef tenderloin, trimmed and tied with kitchen twine in 2-inch sections

1 tablespoon extra-virgin olive oil

Kosher salt and freshly ground black pepper

4 cloves garlic, minced

1 tablespoon chopped fresh rosemary

1 tablespoon chopped fresh thyme

Mashed Potatoes (page 214) and cooked green beans, for serving

1. Preheat the oven to 275°F. Line a baking sheet with foil and coat with cooking spray.

2. Pat the beef dry with paper towels. Drizzle with the oil. Season all over with salt and pepper, then rub all over with the garlic, rosemary, and thyme.

3. Place the beef on the prepared baking sheet and roast until the meat reaches an internal temperature of at least 130° to 135°F for medium-rare, 50 minutes to 1 hour 15 minutes.

4. Transfer the beef to a cutting board and let rest for 10 minutes before slicing. Serve with mashed potatoes and green beans.

Easy Slow Cooker Pork Loin

MAKES 15 TO 20 SERVINGS

PREP TIME:
10 minutes

COOK TIME:
8 hours 6 minutes

Here's another one that is so easy and perfect for those chilly winter nights when you just don't feel like cooking but need a hearty, comforting meal! Pork loin in the slow cooker comes out amazingly tender and juicy, with almost no prep time. Season it, sear it, and toss it in the slow cooker, and dinner is DONE!

1 (5-pound) pork loin, trimmed

1½ tablespoons sea salt

½ teaspoon freshly ground black pepper

1 tablespoon garlic powder

1 tablespoon Italian seasoning

1 teaspoon yellow mustard

1 teaspoon onion powder

10 ounces baby carrots

1 large yellow onion, cut into large pieces

1 cup unsweetened apple juice

1. Pat the pork dry with paper towels. In a small bowl, combine the salt, pepper, garlic powder, Italian seasoning, mustard, and onion powder. Rub the mixture all over the pork.

2. Heat a large skillet over medium-high heat and let it get very hot. Add the pork to the hot pan and sear until browned on both sides, about 3 minutes per side.

3. Add the carrots and onion pieces to a 4- to 6-quart slow cooker and arrange the seared pork loin on top. Pour in the apple juice. Cover and cook on Low for 8 hours or High for 4 hours, until the meat is tender.

4. Transfer the pork to a cutting board. Shred the meat using two forks or let rest for 15 to 20 minutes before slicing against the grain. Arrange on a platter with the carrots and onion and serve.

Cast-Iron Bone-in Rib Eye

MAKES 3 TO
4 SERVINGS

PREP TIME:
5 minutes

COOK TIME:
25 minutes

This dish is my weakness—I become a foaming-at-the-mouth carnivore ready to take a bite when I smell a rib eye sizzling in butter. I have steak once a week and have gone through phases of wanting it every other day. My favorite cut of meat is the rib eye, and I want it bone-in because it's more flavorful that way.

This rib eye pairs nicely with my Spiced Skillet Potatoes (page 120), and one bone-in rib eye, about 8 ounces of meat per person, is good for two people.

1 (1½-pound) bone-in rib eye steak, about 2 inches thick

Sea salt and freshly ground black pepper

1 tablespoon extra-virgin olive oil

3 tablespoons unsalted butter

3 cloves garlic

¼ teaspoon garlic powder

3 sprigs fresh rosemary

1. Preheat the oven to 450°F. Pat the steak dry with paper towels. Season all over with salt and pepper and drizzle with the oil.

2. Heat a cast-iron skillet over medium-high heat until very hot, 1 to 2 minutes. Place the steak in the center of the pan and cook, turning every 2 minutes, until it has a nice dark crust, 8 to 10 minutes.

3. Reduce the heat to medium and move the steak to one side of the pan. Add the butter and garlic and season with salt, pepper, and the garlic powder. Place the rosemary sprigs on the other side of the pan and let the butter melt and foam. Continue cooking, carefully tilting the skillet and spooning the butter over the steak a few times to baste, 1 to 2 minutes more.

4. Once there's a nice char on the steak, transfer it to the oven and cook until the meat reaches an internal temperature of 120°F for medium rare or to your desired doneness, 8 to 10 minutes.

5. Transfer the steak to a cutting board and let rest for 15 minutes before slicing against the grain to serve.

Chicken and Corn Rice Bowls

MAKES 2 SERVINGS

PREP TIME:
15 minutes

COOK TIME:
25 minutes

This is another meal that's perfect for those nights when you want something healthy and filling without a lot of effort. The chicken absorbs all of those slow-cooked flavors from the enchilada simmer sauce and a hint of sweetness from the pineapple salsa. Layer it with your favorite rice (brown, white, or cauliflower), top it with roasted corn and peppers, and enjoy!

1 cup long-grain white rice

1 tablespoon extra-virgin olive oil

1 yellow onion, ½ diced and ½ sliced

2 cloves garlic, minced

2 cups shredded rotisserie chicken

1 cup pineapple salsa

½ cup enchilada simmer sauce

1 teaspoon garlic powder

¼ teaspoon chili powder

¼ teaspoon ground cumin

¼ teaspoon paprika

½ cup frozen white kernel corn

1 red bell pepper, sliced into strips

1 yellow bell pepper, sliced into strips

1 cup shredded Mexican cheese blend

½ avocado, sliced

2 tablespoons chopped fresh cilantro

Lime wedges, for serving

1. Prepare the rice according to the package directions and set aside.

2. Meanwhile, in a large skillet, heat the oil over medium heat. Add the diced onion and the garlic and cook until translucent, about 5 minutes. Add the shredded chicken, salsa, enchilada sauce, garlic powder, chili powder, cumin, and paprika. Stir well to combine. Increase the heat to medium-high, bring to a simmer, and cook for 5 minutes to give the flavors a chance to meld. Reduce the heat to medium-low to keep warm while you roast the veggies.

3. Preheat the oven to 400°F. Line a baking sheet with foil or parchment paper and arrange the corn, bell pepper strips, and onion slices in an even layer. Roast until the peppers and onions are slightly charred and tender, 10 to 15 minutes, tossing halfway through.

4. When ready to serve, add the shredded cheese to the chicken mixture in the skillet and stir to melt. Divide the rice between two bowls, followed by the chicken mixture and roasted veggies. Top with the avocado, cilantro, and lime wedges.

Good for Ya!

Fried Chicken Sandwiches

MAKES 6 TO
12 SERVINGS

PREP TIME:
1 hour

COOK TIME:
55 minutes

Everyone in my family loves fried chicken. Every. Single. One of us. Even more, we all love these fried chicken sandwiches! There's just nothing better than crispy fried buttermilk chicken on a soft roll slathered with mayo! We skip adding any heat so the kids can enjoy them too, but feel free to add a couple squirts of hot sauce on top. *Yummmm.*

3½ pounds boneless chicken breast, cut into 12 pieces

Buttermilk, for marinating

2 cups all-purpose flour

2 tablespoons garlic powder

2 teaspoons sea salt

¾ teaspoon freshly ground black pepper

¾ teaspoon Old Bay Seasoning

¾ teaspoon smoked paprika

¼ teaspoon onion powder

Peanut or vegetable oil, for frying

TO SERVE

1 (12-count) package Hawaiian rolls

¼ cup mayonnaise

Dill pickle chips

1. Add the chicken pieces to a high-sided deep dish or large bowl and cover with enough buttermilk to fully submerge. Transfer to the refrigerator to marinate for 1 hour.

2. In another large bowl, whisk together the flour, garlic powder, salt, pepper, Old Bay, paprika, and onion powder.

3. Line a baking sheet with a wire rack. Working in batches, remove the chicken from the buttermilk, allowing any excess to drip off, dunk in the flour mixture, and toss to thoroughly coat. Tap off the excess flour and transfer to the prepared baking sheet. Let sit at room temperature for 15 minutes.

4. Meanwhile, add enough oil to a high-sided large cast-iron skillet or Dutch oven to fill by one-third. Heat the oil over medium-high heat until it reaches 350°F.

5. Working with 3 or 4 pieces at a time, fry the chicken, turning a few times, until golden brown and crisp and the internal temperature reaches 165°F, 10 to 14 minutes.

6. To serve, separate the Hawaiian rolls and spread each with some of the mayonnaise. Top with the fried chicken pieces and dill pickle chips. Serve hot!

Stuffed Bell Peppers

MAKES 4 SERVINGS

PREP TIME:
20 minutes

COOK TIME:
1 hour

Stuffed peppers are the easy and healthy one-pan dinner you need in your back pocket for those busy winter nights. These little peppers are protein-packed and veggie-forward, and I use lean ground beef or turkey to keep them low in fat. This is a wholesome, hassle-free dinner that your family will love!

Cooking spray, for the baking dish

1 pound lean ground beef

½ cup cooked white rice

½ cup diced white onion

1 clove garlic, minced

2 teaspoons Worcestershire sauce

½ teaspoon onion powder

¼ teaspoon cayenne pepper (optional)

1 large egg, lightly beaten

Sea salt and freshly ground black pepper

4 bell peppers, any color, tops, seeds, and membranes removed

1 cup shredded mozzarella cheese

1 (8-ounce) can tomato sauce

2 tablespoons chopped fresh parsley

1. Preheat the oven to 350°F. Coat a baking dish large enough to hold the peppers upright with cooking spray.

2. In a large bowl, combine the ground beef, cooked rice, diced onion, garlic, Worcestershire, onion powder, cayenne (if using), and egg. Using your hands or a large wooden spoon, mix well. Season with salt and pepper.

3. Stuff the peppers with the ground beef mixture, leaving a little room at the top. Sprinkle with ½ cup shredded cheese, then cover with the tomato sauce. Arrange in the prepared baking dish and bake until the peppers are tender and the meat is no longer pink, about 1 hour. Top with the remaining ½ cup shredded cheese and the parsley before serving.

Turkey Potpie

MAKES 6 TO 8 SERVINGS

PREP TIME:
20 minutes

COOK TIME:
50 minutes

Nothing says cozy comfort in the fall and winter quite like turkey potpie. It also happens to be a creative way to use all that extra turkey from Thanksgiving. If you don't love turkey, you can, of course, use chicken instead.

For the crust, Marie Callender's is the best time-saver there is. The texture is amazing and the flavor is truly delicious. I recommend serving the potpie with warm buttered rolls.

⅓ cup unsalted butter

1 onion, diced

1 Yukon Gold potato, peeled and diced

½ cup diced carrots

½ cup diced celery

⅓ cup all-purpose flour

1 teaspoon Italian seasoning

¼ teaspoon dried thyme

½ teaspoon garlic powder

½ teaspoon onion powder

Sea salt and freshly ground black pepper

1 cup chicken broth

⅔ cup whole milk

2 cups cubed leftover cooked turkey or chicken

1 cup frozen cut green beans

½ cup peas

2 refrigerated piecrusts

1 large egg beaten with 1 tablespoon whole milk

1. Preheat the oven to 400°F.

2. In a large pot or skillet, melt the butter over medium heat. Add the diced onion, potato, carrots, and celery and cook until tender, 5 to 8 minutes. Sprinkle the flour over the veggies, then add the Italian seasoning, thyme, garlic powder, and onion powder and season with salt and pepper. Continue to cook, stirring constantly, for another 2 minutes.

3. While whisking continuously, pour in the chicken broth, followed by the milk. Keep whisking until the mixture is smooth. Increase the heat to medium-high and let come to a simmer for 1 minute, then remove from the heat. Stir in the turkey, green beans, and peas.

4. Line a 9-inch pie plate with one piecrust. Pour the filling into the crust and brush the edges with some of the egg wash. Top with the second piecrust and pinch the edges to seal. Cut a slit in the center to vent, then brush the top crust with more egg wash.

5. Bake the potpie until the crust is lightly browned and the filling is bubbly, 35 to 40 minutes. If the crust starts to brown too quickly, tent with foil.

9

I don't know about you, but seafood just tastes like summer to me—even when I'm nowhere near a beach or it's the middle of February. Some of my favorite restaurants are seafood places, and I love everything about the fresh flavors. From crab to lobster and even my favorite tuna sandwich, here are some of my favorite fish and seafood recipes!

Under the Sea

Recipes with ○ icon indicate "Good for Ya!" recipes.

Lobster Risotto

MAKES 4 SERVINGS

PREP TIME:
15 minutes

COOK TIME:
40 minutes

Lobster risotto is one of those recipes that intimidates a lot of people, but once you've made it, you'll want it over and over again. This recipe cooks slow and steady to make sure the rice is just right, so have fun with it. Grab a glass of wine, turn on some bossa nova music, and commit to just hanging out by the stove. Trust me when I say this dish is worth the extra time.

1 cooked whole lobster

6 cups chicken broth

4 tablespoons (½ stick) unsalted butter

2 tablespoons extra-virgin olive oil

2 large shallots, finely chopped

5 button mushrooms, sliced

1 cup arborio rice

¾ cup white wine

Chopped fresh parsley, for serving

1. De-shell the lobster and remove the meat from the tail and claws. Cut into chunks and set aside.

2. In a small saucepan, bring the chicken broth to a simmer over medium-high heat, about 5 minutes. Reduce the heat to low to keep warm.

3. In a large pot, heat 2 tablespoons butter and 1 tablespoon oil over medium-high heat. Add the shallots and cook until softened, 5 to 7 minutes. Add the mushrooms and cook until they release their moisture, about 2 minutes.

4. Add the rice, toss to coat well, and cook until toasted, about 3 minutes. Pour in the wine and cook until most of the liquid has been absorbed, about 1 minute. Reduce the heat to medium and add ½ cup of the warm chicken broth, stirring frequently, until it has mostly been absorbed. Continue cooking, adding the broth ½ cup at a time and allowing the rice to mostly absorb it before adding more, until you've used all the broth and the rice is tender, 15 to 20 minutes.

5. Remove from the heat and stir in the remaining 1 tablespoon oil and 2 tablespoons butter, then fold in the lobster meat. Serve garnished with chopped parsley.

Tuna Sangwiches

MAKES 6 TO
8 SERVINGS

PREP TIME:
10 minutes

When I was growing up, my maw-maw, Mary Baglio, used to say "sangwiches" instead of "sandwiches," which I think is really cute. Now my mama, Vivi's maw-maw, says it. So get used to me doing it too!

Each time I was pregnant, I craved tuna and chicken salad sangwiches for some reason. I've always been the girl whose food you don't mess with—and this was even more true when I was preggo. When I was hungry and craving something, I had to have it. I would scarf these tuna sangwiches down with a bag of barbecue chips, and it was the most satisfying thing for a pregnant gal like me.

This recipe is so good. I threw it together one afternoon and Eric loved it. It makes six to eight sangwiches, depending on how much filling you prefer. You can load up on veggies or load up on filling (I like a lot of tuna in my sangwiches!). Some people are funny about tuna, so if you are, either try this or skip to the next page and miss out on some sangwich bomb-ness.

4 (5-ounce) cans water-packed albacore tuna, drained

2 hard-boiled large eggs, diced

1 dill pickle, diced

1 sweet pickle, diced

1 cup avocado oil mayonnaise

1 tablespoon yellow mustard

1 tablespoon chopped fresh dill

1 teaspoon garlic powder

Pinch of Tony Chachere's Creole Seasoning

Salt and freshly ground black pepper

TO SERVE

12 to 16 slices soft white sandwich bread

Green-leaf lettuce

2 tomatoes, sliced

Sweet pickle chips

Barbecue potato chips

1. Add the tuna, eggs, dill pickle, sweet pickle, mayonnaise, mustard, dill, garlic powder, and Tony's seasoning to a large bowl and fold to combine. Season with salt and pepper.

2. For each sangwich, scoop some of the filling onto a slice of bread. Top with lettuce, sliced tomatoes, pickle chips, and another slice of bread. Serve with barbecue chips on the side.

Baja Babe Fish Tacos

MAKES 8 SERVINGS

PREP TIME:
20 minutes

COOK TIME:
25 minutes

Fried fish tacos are the taco of choice on vacation, with shrimp tacos a close second. I have had many styles of fried fish taco and, not surprisingly, they do it best in Mexico! The breading has to be crispy and perfectly seasoned. Here is my version, hopefully perfected after lots of trips to Cabo and Cancun.

FOR THE SAUCE

⅓ cup sour cream

½ cup avocado oil mayonnaise

Juice of 1 lime

¼ teaspoon garlic powder

¼ teaspoon chipotle powder

FOR THE FISH

1 cup all-purpose flour

1 teaspoon cayenne pepper (optional, for some heat)

1 teaspoon garlic powder

½ teaspoon baking powder

½ teaspoon salt, plus more for sprinkling

⅔ cup Mexican lager, plus more as needed

Oil, for frying

1 pound firm white fish, preferably cod or halibut, cut into 16 pieces

TO SERVE

2 cups finely shredded cabbage

8 corn tortillas, warmed or fried

1 avocado, thinly sliced

Jalapeño slices (optional, for some heat)

Shredded Mexican cheese blend

¼ cup chopped fresh cilantro

Lime wedges

1. Make the sauce: In a small bowl, whisk together the sour cream, mayonnaise, lime juice, garlic powder, and chipotle powder. Refrigerate until ready to use.

2. Make the fish: In a large bowl, whisk together the flour, cayenne (if using), garlic powder, baking powder, and salt. Pour in the beer and whisk until the mixture has the consistency of batter. If it seems too thick, add more beer a splash at a time until you reach the desired consistency.

3. Add enough oil to a large pot to fill by 3 inches. Turn the heat to medium-high and heat the oil until it reaches 350°F.

4. Pat the fish pieces dry with paper towels and dip in the batter to coat completely. Working in batches of two or three pieces at a time, add the fish to the hot oil and fry until golden, 2 to 3 minutes. As each batch finishes frying, transfer the fish to paper towels to drain and sprinkle with a bit of salt.

5. For each taco, add some of the shredded cabbage to a warm tortilla. Add two pieces of fried fish; top with avocado slices, jalapeño slices (if using), shredded cheese, and chopped cilantro; and drizzle with the sauce. Serve with lime wedges on the side for squeezing.

Pan-Seared Grouper with Tomato Jam

MAKES 2 SERVINGS

PREP TIME:
2 hours

COOK TIME:
10 minutes

Fish can be a finicky piece of meat to cook. It can get too dry or too tough, or end up flavorless. But not with this recipe! I love to pan-sear in a little butter and oil to really lock in the juices for the most flavorful and flaky fish you'll ever have. I serve it over a bed of white rice and top it off with some homemade tomato jam.

FOR THE TOMATO JAM

2 pounds Roma tomatoes, cored and cut into 1-inch pieces

2 tablespoons apple cider vinegar

¼ cup packed dark brown sugar

1 teaspoon sea salt

½ teaspoon ground cumin

¼ teaspoon ground ginger

¼ teaspoon smoked paprika

¼ teaspoon crushed red pepper flakes

FOR THE GROUPER

2 (6-ounce) red grouper fillets

Salt and freshly ground black pepper

1 tablespoon coconut oil

2 tablespoons unsalted butter

2 sprigs thyme, plus more for garnish

1 tablespoon fresh lemon juice

1 cup cooked jasmine rice, for serving

1. Make the tomato jam (see note): Add the tomatoes, vinegar, brown sugar, salt, cumin, ginger, paprika, and pepper flakes to a medium pot or Dutch oven over medium-high heat. Let the mixture come to a low boil, stirring occasionally, about 5 minutes. Once boiling, reduce the heat to medium and simmer until thickened to a jam consistency, about 2 hours. Transfer to a mason jar and set aside to cool while you prepare the fish.

2. Make the fish: Pat the fish dry with paper towels. Season on both sides with salt and pepper.

3. Heat a heavy 10-inch nonstick or cast-iron skillet over high heat. When the pan is hot, add the oil.

4. Place the fish in the pan and reduce the heat to medium. Cook until caramelized around the edges, 2 to 3 minutes. Carefully flip and add the butter and thyme to the pan. Add the lemon juice, then tilt the pan to pull the melted butter to one side. Use a spoon to baste the fish with the melted butter. Continue basting and cooking until golden and cooked through, 2 to 3 minutes more, depending on the thickness of your fish.

5. To serve, divide the rice between plates and top with the grouper, followed by a generous scoop of tomato jam and fresh thyme.

Jessie's note:

The tomato jam can be made ahead and stored in the fridge for up to two weeks. It's delicious on burgers, as part of a cheese board, and just about anywhere else you might use a spread.

Shrimp Tacos

MAKES 6 SERVINGS

PREP TIME:
15 minutes

COOK TIME:
10 minutes

Shrimp tacos are my second favorite way to eat seafood. I love the texture of the cool, crispy shredded cabbage and the perfectly cooked shrimp all wrapped up in a warm tortilla. These shrimp tacos are light on calories and full of fiber! Use corn or flour tortillas depending on what you like, and don't forget the frosty margs and guac to go with the theme.

FOR THE SAUCE AND SLAW

½ cup sour cream

3 tablespoons mayonnaise

Juice of 1 lime

½ teaspoon ground cumin

¼ teaspoon garlic powder

¼ teaspoon sea salt

¼ teaspoon freshly ground black pepper

3 cups finely shredded green cabbage

½ small red onion, sliced

3 tablespoons chopped fresh cilantro

FOR THE TACOS

1 teaspoon chili powder

1 teaspoon ground cumin

1 teaspoon sea salt

½ teaspoon onion powder

½ teaspoon garlic powder

1 pound shrimp, peeled and deveined, tails removed

Juice of ½ lime, plus wedges for serving

2 tablespoons extra-virgin olive oil

6 corn or flour tortillas

Green tomatillo salsa and chopped fresh cilantro, for serving

1. Make the sauce and slaw: In a small bowl, whisk together the sour cream, mayonnaise, lime juice, cumin, garlic powder, salt, and pepper. In a medium bowl, toss together the cabbage, onion, and cilantro. Add about half of the sauce to the slaw and toss to coat (save the rest of the sauce for serving). Set aside.

2. Make the tacos: In a large bowl, combine the chili powder, cumin, salt, onion powder, and garlic powder. Add the shrimp and the lime juice. Toss to coat.

3. In a large skillet, heat the oil over medium heat. Add the shrimp and cook, turning once, until pink, 2 to 3 minutes on each side. Transfer to a serving dish.

4. In another large skillet over medium-high heat, warm the tortillas in batches of two or three, turning occasionally.

5. To assemble the tacos, on top of each tortilla add a layer of cabbage slaw followed by shrimp. Top with salsa and cilantro. Serve with lime wedges and the remaining sauce on the side.

Good for Ya!

Crab-Stuffed Mushrooms

MAKES 10 TO 12 SERVINGS

PREP TIME:
10 minutes

COOK TIME:
20 minutes

Anytime I make these stuffed mushrooms they disappear. Every bite has a mix of creamy crab and zesty seasoned bread crumbs with a little hint of Louisiana hot sauce. These are the perfect size for a two-bite appetizer your guests will love.

5 ounces cream cheese, softened

¼ cup grated Parmesan cheese, plus more for garnish

2 cloves garlic, minced

2 tablespoons chopped fresh parsley, plus more for garnish

1 tablespoon chopped fresh chives

½ teaspoon salt

½ teaspoon freshly ground black pepper

¼ teaspoon Louisiana hot sauce

8 ounces lump crabmeat

½ cup seasoned bread crumbs

1 tablespoon extra-virgin olive oil

20 button or baby bella mushrooms, stemmed

Olive oil cooking spray, for the mushrooms

1. Preheat the oven to 375°F. Line a baking sheet with foil.

2. In a large bowl, mix the cream cheese, Parmesan, garlic, parsley, chives, salt, pepper, and hot sauce. Fold in the crabmeat. In a small bowl, stir together the bread crumbs and oil.

3. Spritz the mushrooms with cooking spray. Fill the mushroom cavities with rounded tablespoons of the crabmeat filling, enough to create a dome. Carefully roll in the bread crumbs to coat and arrange, cavity side up, on the prepared baking sheet. Bake until the mushrooms are tender and the filling is heated through and golden on top, about 20 minutes. Garnish with chopped parsley and grated Parmesan cheese to serve.

Shrimp Fried Rice

MAKES 4 TO 6 SERVINGS

PREP TIME:
10 minutes

COOK TIME:
20 minutes

Why get takeout when you can make a delicious shrimp fried rice at home? This recipe is perfect when I've got to get dinner made and I want to use up fresh veggies or leftover rice. Feel free to add sesame oil in place of avocado oil if that's your thing, but at the Decker house we avoid it due to Vivi's allergy.

1 cup broccoli florets

3 tablespoons avocado oil

1 red bell pepper, cut into thin strips

1 yellow bell pepper, cut into thin strips

1½ cups frozen edamame, thawed

1 cup sugar snap peas, trimmed and halved crosswise

1 cup cooked white rice

1 teaspoon ground ginger

12 ounces medium shrimp, peeled and deveined

¼ cup low-sodium soy sauce, plus more for serving

1½ tablespoons rice vinegar

1 teaspoon Sriracha, plus more for serving

¼ cup thinly sliced scallions

2 large eggs, beaten

1. Using a steamer or a medium pot fitted with a steamer basket, steam the broccoli until crisp-tender, about 4 minutes. Set aside.

2. Heat a large skillet or wok over medium-high heat. Add 1 teaspoon avocado oil to the pan. Once shimmering, add the bell peppers, edamame, and snap peas and stir-fry for 2 minutes. Transfer the vegetables to a large bowl.

3. Add 2 tablespoons avocado oil to the same pan. Add the cooked rice and ginger and stir-fry until the rice is lightly browned, about 5 minutes. Transfer to the bowl with the vegetables. Wipe out the pan.

4. Add the remaining avocado oil to the same pan over medium-high heat. Add the shrimp and stir-fry until slightly pink, 1 to 2 minutes. Pour in the soy sauce, vinegar, and Sriracha and simmer until the liquid begins to thicken, about 3 minutes. Add the broccoli, rice mixture, and scallions and stir to combine. Add the eggs and stir continuously to scramble. Continue cooking, stirring frequently, until heated through, about 2 minutes. Serve with extra Sriracha and soy sauce on the side.

10

Kids' meals don't have to be just for kids! These recipes are what my kids love to eat and what I feel good about feeding them. Whether it's homemade chicken tenders or their favorite granola bars, I love cooking foods that the whole family can enjoy and get involved in.

My kids love to help in the kitchen, and all the recipes in this chapter are ones that your little ones can assist with here and there. Having them stir, measure, or sprinkle ingredients is a great way to make them part of the experience, and they'll eat better when they help too!

Kids' Meals
They'll Actually Love

Yaya's Hot Dogs and Mash

MAKES 6 SERVINGS

PREP TIME:
15 minutes

COOK TIME:
15 minutes

My grandmother, whom I call Yaya (she's Greek), used to make these hot dogs, one of my favorite meals when I was growing up. It's not a Greek dish, but I sure did love it, and now my kids love it too. It's so simple to put hot dogs and mashed potatoes together, and it's also so good.

5 large russet potatoes, peeled and halved (see note)

Sea salt and freshly ground black pepper

4 tablespoons (½ stick) unsalted butter

¼ cup 2 percent or whole milk

1 (10-ounce) package all-beef hot dogs (see note)

½ cup shredded Cheddar cheese (optional)

1. Preheat the oven to 350°F and line a baking sheet with foil or parchment paper.

2. Add the potatoes to a large pot and pour in enough water to completely cover them. Season generously with salt. Bring to a boil and cook until fork tender, about 15 minutes. Drain and return the potatoes to the pot.

3. Using a potato masher, mash the potatoes roughly. Add the butter and fold in until melted. Pour in the milk and continue mashing until very smooth. Season generously with salt and pepper.

4. Using a sharp knife, make a lengthwise slit down the center of each hot dog, being careful not to cut all the way through. Stuff each hot dog with enough of the mashed potatoes to overflow a bit.

5. Arrange the stuffed hot dogs on the prepared baking sheet and bake until heated through, about 10 minutes. If you'd like to make them extra fancy, top with the Cheddar and broil until the cheese melts, 1 to 3 minutes.

Jessie's note:

If you can get them, we like all-beef hot dogs that skip the fillers and artificial colors or flavors. You can also use leftover mashed potatoes for this meal, which makes it a quick and easy one for those busy nights when you don't have a lot of time to cook the potatoes.

Homemade DIY Snack Mix

MAKES 13 CUPS

PREP TIME:
15 minutes

There isn't much to this snack mix, but what I think makes it special is the *process*. It's less of a recipe and more of an activity I do with the kids on their own or when their friends come over. I like to set up a bunch of little bowls and fill each one up with different things so the kids can customize their mix in a personalized zip-top bag.

4 cups Chex cereal of choice

2 cups mini pretzels

2 cups Goldfish crackers

1 cup raisins

1 cup M&M's

1 cup Reese's Pieces

2 cups mini marshmallows

Powdered sugar

1. Gather enough bowls for each of the ingredients you want to include and fill them with your goodies. Put little spoons in each bowl and give kids their own zip-top bag to make their mix the way they like it.

2. Once kids are finished filling their bags, add a spoonful of powdered sugar to each bag and zip it up. Have them shake it all together. (This gets them so excited!) Add each kid's name to their bag and let them enjoy!

Kids' Cheese Boards

MAKES 4 KID
SERVINGS

PREP TIME:
10 minutes

One thing my kids crave is their own little cheese board like the adults have. Sometimes for a snack or when I'm preparing a meal, I'll grab some of these little mini wood boards I found at Trader Joe's and make a small arrangement of fruits, cheese, and crackers for each kid. They absolutely love it. They can each have whatever items they want on their board, and they can put it all together like homemade Lunchables. It's those little things that don't take too much effort that make mealtime special and memorable.

1 sleeve Ritz crackers (about 32 crackers)

1 cup raisins

4 ounces Cheddar cheese

4 ounces BellaVitano cheese, any type you like

½ cup sliced sausage or pepperoni

1 cup blueberries

1 cup sliced strawberries

Honey, for serving (optional)

Arrange the crackers, raisins, cheeses, sausage, blueberries, and strawberries on individual mini wooden serving boards for the kids to enjoy! Serve with individual mini dishes of honey if desired.

Granola Bars

MAKES 8 SERVINGS

PREP TIME:
15 minutes

CHILL TIME:
1 hour

My babies love granola bars more than anyone I know, and while they love all kinds, their fave is any type of oatmeal chocolate chip bar they can get their little hands on. Of course, it's easier to buy a box of granola bars and hand them out that way—but I think they taste better from scratch, especially with your little ones helping. It's a special activity to do with your kids.

2 cups rolled oats

1 cup oat flour

¼ cup brown sugar

½ teaspoon baking soda

½ teaspoon salt

½ cup honey

¼ cup coconut oil, melted

¼ cup applesauce

2 teaspoons pure vanilla extract

1 cup milk or dark chocolate chips

1. Line an 8-inch baking pan with parchment paper. In a large bowl, combine the rolled oats, oat flour, brown sugar, baking soda, and salt. In a separate large bowl, whisk together the honey, coconut oil, applesauce, and vanilla. Stir the wet ingredients into the dry ingredients. Fold in the chocolate chips.

2. Transfer to the prepared pan and smooth it out with a silicone spatula or by placing a piece of parchment paper on top and pressing down as hard as you can.

3. Let chill in the refrigerator until firm, about 1 hour. Slice into 8 bars to serve. Keep refrigerated up to 1 week.

Healthier Cheesy Hamburger Mac

MAKES 6 SERVINGS

PREP TIME:
10 minutes

COOK TIME:
20 minutes

Pasta in a creamy, cheesy meat sauce? Yes, please. But this recipe isn't like your average box of Hamburger Helper. It's got healthy whole-food ingredients and a secret nutrition boost from hidden chopped carrots. Not only will kids eat it all, but they won't even realize it has veggies!

2 tablespoons extra-virgin olive oil

1 yellow onion, chopped

½ cup finely chopped carrot

1 pound lean ground beef

Sea salt and freshly ground black pepper

1 teaspoon chili powder

1 teaspoon paprika

1 teaspoon garlic powder

2 cups unsweetened almond milk

1 tablespoon ketchup

2 teaspoons Worcestershire sauce

1 teaspoon yellow mustard

1 pound pasta, such as small shells, elbow macaroni, or rigatoni

1½ to 2 cups shredded Cheddar cheese

Chopped fresh parsley, for serving

1. In a large skillet, heat the oil over medium-high heat. Add the onion and carrot and cook until just softened, 5 minutes. Add the ground beef, season with salt and pepper, and cook, breaking up the meat with a wooden spoon, until browned, about 7 minutes. Add the chili powder, paprika, and garlic powder and cook, stirring, for 1 minute. Add the almond milk, ketchup, Worcestershire, and mustard and stir to combine. Season with a little salt and reduce the heat to medium. Keep at a simmer while you prepare the pasta.

2. Meanwhile, in a large pot of salted boiling water, cook the pasta to al dente according to the package directions.

3. Drain the pasta and add to the skillet with the beef mixture. Add the Cheddar and stir until melted and the pasta is coated in a creamy sauce. Serve topped with parsley.

Fairy Cakes

**MAKES ABOUT
24 CUPCAKES**

PREP TIME:
15 minutes

REST TIME:
1 hour

COOK TIME:
25 minutes

This is a recipe that my aunt used to make, and it's just one of the cutest ways to make cupcakes. It starts off with a box of yellow cake mix plus a little flavoring to make it extra special. After the cupcakes are finished and have cooled, you cut the tops off and arrange them just right to look like fairy wings. It's such a unique cupcake that doubles as a fun activity for the kids to help with.

If you don't love the idea of regular boxed cake mix, there are tons of healthier cake mixes that you can buy. You could even make gluten-free or sugar-free cupcakes if that's what you need!

½ teaspoon almond extract

½ teaspoon pure vanilla extract

1 box yellow cake mix, prepared according to the package directions

1 cup heavy whipping cream

1 (12-ounce) jar raspberry jam (you won't use it all)

Powdered sugar, for dusting

1. Preheat the oven to 350°F and fill two cupcake pans with enough paper liners for 24 cupcakes.

2. In a large bowl, add the almond and vanilla extracts to the prepared batter. Fill each cupcake liner about halfway with batter. Bake until a toothpick inserted in the center of a cupcake comes out clean, about 25 minutes. Let cool to room temperature, about 1 hour.

3. Using a sharp knife, cut a circle from the top of each cupcake at a 45-degree angle. Slice each circle in half—these will be the fairy wings.

4. Whip the heavy cream to soft peaks and place a dollop on each cupcake. Arrange the two halves of the circle on top to resemble fairy wings, followed by a dollop of jam in the center. Dust with powdered sugar.

Homemade Chicken Tenders

MAKES 4 SERVINGS

PREP TIME:
10 minutes

COOK TIME:
16 minutes

I know it's easier to pop some frozen nuggets into the oven, but I won't eat them like that, and I don't love it for my kids either. These chicken tenders really don't take that long, and they're much tastier and better for everyone. Serve these with their favorite veggies or oven baked fries. Let's dive in!

½ cup all-purpose flour

1 teaspoon paprika

½ teaspoon garlic powder

Salt and freshly ground black pepper

2 large eggs

¾ cup panko bread crumbs

1 pound chicken breast tenders

¼ cup extra-virgin olive oil

Shredded Parmesan cheese, for serving (optional)

Dipping sauces, for serving

1. In a shallow bowl, combine the flour with the paprika, garlic powder, and salt and pepper. In a second shallow bowl, lightly beat the eggs. Place the panko in a third shallow bowl.

2. Coat the chicken in the flour mixture, then dip in the beaten eggs, then roll in the panko.

3. In a large skillet, heat 2 tablespoons oil over medium heat. Add half the chicken and cook, flipping once, until golden brown and cooked through, about 4 minutes on each side. Transfer to a paper towel–lined plate. Repeat with the remaining 2 tablespoons oil and chicken.

4. Serve the chicken tenders sprinkled with some Parmesan (if your kids are into that) and whatever dipping sauces your babies like.

Chicken and Corn Quesadillas

MAKES 6 TO 8 SERVINGS

PREP TIME:
10 minutes

COOK TIME:
1 hour

I'm all about easy and quick meals that also happen to be delicious. This one is so flavorful that my kids are always happy to see it on the dinner table, but it is definitely a fancier way to serve your kids quesadillas. Mine are used to interesting and sometimes unexpected meals, and if I tried to serve them a tortilla with melted cheese, they would probably look at me like I forgot something!

Serve these quesadillas with toppings like salsa, sour cream, and Eric's Guacamole (you can find that recipe in my last book, *Just Feed Me*). The kids love when I serve each topping in a mini bowl so they can have their choice for dipping. I've found it's the little things that make meals fun and interactive.

2 tablespoons avocado oil

¼ cup diced onion

¼ cup chopped red bell pepper

¼ cup chopped green bell pepper

1 cup frozen fire-roasted corn

2 cloves garlic, minced

3 cups shredded rotisserie chicken

⅛ teaspoon fine sea salt

Softened butter, for the tortillas

8 (8-inch) flour tortillas

4 cups shredded Mexican cheese blend

Sour cream, guacamole, and salsa, for serving

1. In a large skillet, heat the oil over medium heat. Add the onion, bell peppers, and corn and cook, stirring, until tender, 5 to 7 minutes. Add the garlic and cook until fragrant, about 1 minute. Add the chicken, season with the salt, and toss to combine. Reduce the heat to medium-low and cook until the chicken is heated through, 10 minutes.

2. Heat another large skillet over medium heat. Butter both sides of a tortilla and add to the pan. Spoon some of the chicken mixture onto half of the tortilla and top with a handful of cheese. Fold the other half of the tortilla over the filling and cook, flipping once, until browned on both sides and the cheese is melted, 3 to 5 minutes per side. Repeat with the remaining tortillas, chicken mixture, and cheese.

3. Serve the quesadillas with sour cream, guacamole, and salsa for dipping.

11

The holidays are all about building traditions. When I was a kid, my mom went all out with decorations and special meals that filled our house with lots of happiness and love. These are the recipes that I make for my family to continue these traditions, plus some new ones that we've added over the years.

Home for the Holidays

Spiked Apple Cider

MAKES 6 TO
8 SERVINGS

PREP TIME:
5 minutes

CHILL TIME:
30 minutes

It's not a holiday without a fun and festive cocktail! Spiked apple cider is one of my favorite ways to get in the spirit. I serve it cold over ice, but there's plenty of booze to warm you up on a chilly Thanksgiving or Christmas day!

4 cups apple cider

½ cup dark rum

½ cup cinnamon schnapps

1 Granny Smith apple, peeled, cored, and cut into large chunks, plus more apple slices for serving

Pinch of ground cinnamon, plus more for serving

Ice

Cinnamon sticks, for serving

Rosemary sprigs, for serving

1. In a large pitcher, combine the cider, rum, and schnapps.

2. Add the apples and cinnamon and stir. Refrigerate for 30 minutes.

3. To serve, pour the spiked cider into cocktail glasses filled with ice, then garnish with cinnamon sticks, rosemary, and an apple slice. Sprinkle with cinnamon.

Pumpkin Spice Latte

MAKES 1 LATTE

PREP TIME:
15 minutes

COOK TIME:
5 minutes

Nothing says fall more than a pumpkin spice latte! But I will admit, the ones at the chain coffee shops are too sweet for me and filled with too many strange ingredients. Still, I love the flavor, so when a craving hit me, I decided to create my own. It's super easy and absolutely delicious, and it will warm your heart on a perfect autumn day.

¾ cup unsweetened almond milk, or milk of choice

2 tablespoons pure pumpkin puree

2 teaspoons pure maple syrup

½ teaspoon pumpkin pie spice

1 teaspoon pure vanilla extract

½ cup strong brewed black coffee

Ground cinnamon, for serving

1. In a small saucepan, combine the milk, pumpkin puree, maple syrup, and pumpkin pie spice and warm over medium heat, whisking, until just simmering, 3 to 5 minutes. Turn off the heat and add the vanilla.

2. Transfer the warm milk mixture to a large bowl and froth with a milk frother or an immersion blender. (This is the secret to creating a homemade latte without the fancy machine. If you don't have either of these tools, you can use a blender.)

3. Pour the frothed milk into a large coffee mug, then add the brewed coffee. Serve with a little cinnamon sprinkled on top.

Butterscotch Haystacks

**MAKES 18 TO
24 PIECES**

PREP TIME:
5 minutes

COOK TIME:
5 minutes

CHILL TIME:
2 hours

I had these for the first time in Denver at a friend's house. I wanted to eat them all, but we had just become friends and I didn't want her to think I was rude! Well, now I make them myself and will practically finish a whole platter. These are a perfect fall treat that you can make with the kids. I love the butterscotch flavor and the crunch. They're great to share with your neighbors and teachers in a cute little Halloween- or autumn-themed baggie.

1 cup butterscotch chips

½ cup creamy peanut butter

1½ cups chow mein noodles

1. Line a baking sheet with wax paper.

2. In a medium saucepan, melt the butterscotch chips over low heat until smooth, 3 to 4 minutes.

3. Remove from the heat and stir in the peanut butter until well combined. Add the chow mein noodles and stir gently to combine.

4. Drop rounded tablespoons of the mixture onto the prepared baking sheet. Let the haystacks firm up in the fridge or at room temperature for at least 2 hours. They'll keep for a week stored in an airtight container in the fridge (for a firmer haystack) or at room temperature (for a softer texture).

Apple Cider Doughnuts

MAKES ABOUT
A DOZEN
DOUGHNUTS

PREP TIME:
15 minutes

CHILL TIME:
1 hour

COOK TIME:
1 hour

Fall is my favorite time of year. I love the food and festivities! I get so excited about all the chili, pumpkin cookies, and apple cider doughnuts. I don't love baking because it's complex, but this recipe is easy even for me. Y'all will love this.

3 cups apple cider

3½ cups all-purpose flour, plus more for rolling

⅔ cup packed brown sugar

2 teaspoons baking powder

¾ teaspoon salt

½ teaspoon baking soda

¼ teaspoon ground cardamom

¼ teaspoon ground nutmeg

¼ teaspoon ground cinnamon

¼ teaspoon allspice

2 large eggs, lightly beaten

6 tablespoons unsalted butter, melted and cooled

Canola oil, for frying

½ cup cinnamon sugar

1. In a medium saucepan, bring the cider to a boil over high heat. Reduce the heat to medium-high and cook until reduced by half, 12 to 15 minutes. Remove from the heat and let cool completely.

2. In a large bowl, whisk together the flour, brown sugar, baking powder, salt, baking soda, cardamom, nutmeg, cinnamon, and allspice.

3. In a separate large bowl whisk together the eggs, butter, and cooled cider until blended.

4. Create a well in the center of the flour mixture. Pour the wet ingredients into the well and begin mixing from inside the well to the outer edges until a sticky dough forms (just like when making homemade pasta). Cover the dough with a towel and chill for 1 hour.

5. When ready to fry, place the dough on a lightly floured work surface and roll out to a ½-inch-thick round. Cut out doughnuts using a floured doughnut cutter. Arrange the doughnuts and doughnut holes on a baking sheet.

6. To fry, fill a deep pot with enough oil to cover by about 4 inches. Heat the oil until it reaches 350°F. Working in batches of 2 or 3, fry the doughnuts, turning, until golden brown, 2 to 3 minutes on each side. Fry the doughnut holes, turning, until golden brown, 1 minute per side. Transfer the fried doughnuts to a paper towel–lined plate and coat in the cinnamon sugar.

Thanksgiving Turkey

**MAKES 8 TO
10 SERVINGS**

PREP TIME:
20 minutes

COOK TIME:
3 to 5 hours

A turkey is usually the star of the show on Thanksgiving, so it's important to make sure you season it well and butter it up for a tender and flavorful bird! Here's my simple, no-fuss prep for the perfect centerpiece to your holiday feast.

1 (12- to 20-pound)
 turkey

Sea salt and freshly
 ground black
 pepper

1 white onion,
 quartered

3 whole carrots,
 trimmed, peeled,
 and quartered

1 apple, quartered

1 bundle poultry
 herbs (2 sprigs
 each thyme,
 rosemary, and
 sage)

8 tablespoons
 (1 stick) butter,
 melted

1. Preheat the oven to 325°F. Place the turkey on a clean work surface. Pull the neck and giblets out of the cavity; discard the liver and save the rest of the giblets for gravy if desired. Pat the turkey dry with paper towels, then season generously inside and out with salt and pepper.

2. Fill the turkey with the onion, carrots, apple, and herb bundle, then place it breast side up in a roasting pan. Brush the bird all over with half the melted butter. Tent with foil and roast for 2 hours for a 12-pound turkey; for larger birds, add an extra 15 minutes of roasting time per pound.

3. Remove the turkey from the oven and baste with the remaining melted butter. Increase the oven temperature to 425°F. Return the turkey to the oven and roast until the meat reaches an internal temperature of 165°F, about 1 hour. Let rest for 20 minutes before carving or making gravy.

Roasted Rack of Lamb

MAKES 8 SERVINGS

PREP TIME:
1 hour 10 minutes

COOK TIME:
30 minutes

Rack of lamb is one of those recipes that scares a lot of people, but it's really an easy dish that is perfect for a holiday meal. Whether it's Easter Sunday or a big Christmas dinner, this lamb will wow your guests and have them thinking you're a five-star chef.

2 (1½-pound) racks of lamb, trimmed of all but a thin layer of fat

3 tablespoons extra-virgin olive oil

1½ teaspoons sea salt

¾ teaspoon freshly ground black pepper

3 cloves garlic, minced, plus 6 whole cloves

2 tablespoons chopped fresh rosemary, plus a few springs for garnish

2 tablespoons Dijon mustard

2 teaspoons honey

1. Place the racks of lamb on a foil-lined baking sheet. Drizzle with 1 tablespoon oil and season with the salt and pepper.

2. In a small bowl, combine the garlic, rosemary, Dijon mustard, remaining 2 tablespoons oil, and the honey. Coat the meat completely in this mixture. Arrange the garlic cloves on a baking sheet and lay the lamb on top. Let it marinate in the refrigerator for 1 hour.

3. Preheat the oven to 450°F.

4. Roast the lamb until the meat reaches an internal temperature of 145°F, about 30 minutes. Remove from the oven and let it rest for 10 minutes before slicing. Serve with roasted garlic and fresh rosemary.

Christmas Wreath Salad

MAKES 4 TO 6 SERVINGS

PREP TIME: 15 minutes

I've been making this salad for years now. It's a family and friend favorite because of its delicious Christmassy flavor and festive appearance. You will need a round platter, so you can shape the salad into a wreath and add extra dressing in a small bowl in the middle. This is perfect for Christmas parties.

FOR THE DRESSING

- 1/4 cup apple cider vinegar
- 3 tablespoons extra-virgin olive oil
- 1 1/2 tablespoons pure maple syrup
- 1 teaspoon fresh lemon juice
- 1 teaspoon Dijon mustard
- Pinch each of sea salt and freshly ground black pepper

FOR THE SALAD

- 6 to 8 cups mixed greens
- 1 red apple, cored and sliced
- 1/2 small red onion, sliced
- 3/4 cup pomegranate seeds
- 1/2 cup chopped pecans
- 3 ounces goat cheese (or feta if you're not a fan of goat cheese)

1. Make the dressing: In a small bowl, whisk together the vinegar, oil, syrup, lemon juice, and Dijon. Season with salt and pepper.

2. Make the salad: In a large bowl, toss together the mixed greens, apple, onion, 1/2 cup pomegranate seeds, and the pecans. Add half the dressing and toss to coat.

3. Transfer the dressed salad to a round serving platter and form into a wreath shape. Crumble the goat cheese on top and sprinkle with the remaining 1/4 cup pomegranate seeds for that extra red pop. Place the small bowl with the remaining dressing in the center of the wreath.

Cranberry-Brie Pull-Apart Bread

MAKES 6 TO
8 SERVINGS

PREP TIME:
20 minutes

COOK TIME:
20 minutes

It was around Christmas, and I had two loaves of French bread that I had planned to slice up, toast, and drizzle with olive oil as a quick little appetizer. But then I remembered a recipe a friend had told me about that included French bread and cheese. For some reason, brie is the one cheese that goes untouched when I put it on my charcuterie boards. I can't seem to figure out why. I love brie! I had two packages of it in my fridge, and I decided to look up if I could melt the brie over the bread. I started coming across all these delicious brie bread recipes, and I decided to try a combo of a few I had found. Over the years, the recipe I came up with has become a family favorite. I guarantee there will be absolutely none left, and you will be filled with joy watching people lick their fingers—it's that delicious.

1 round loaf French bread

1 cup dried cranberries

2/3 cup pecans, chopped

4 tablespoons (1/2 stick) unsalted butter

3 tablespoons brown sugar

1 tablespoon orange zest plus 1 tablespoon fresh juice

1 (16-ounce) wheel brie cheese, cubed

1/2 cup shredded mozzarella cheese

1. Preheat the oven to 350°F.

2. Slice the bread both horizontally and vertically in 1-inch sections 2 to 3 inches deep to make a grid of 1-inch bread cubes. Do not slice all the way through! The loaf should still be intact.

3. In a small bowl, combine the cranberries, pecans, butter, brown sugar, and orange zest and juice. Using a fork or your hands, mix until crumbly.

4. Place the sliced bread on a baking sheet and stuff with the brie, mozzarella, and cranberry-pecan mixture. Try to fill every crease all the way to the bottom for the best results.

5. Bake until the cheese is melted and gooey, 15 to 20 minutes. Let your guests serve themselves by pulling apart pieces of the bread.

Mashed Potatoes

**MAKES 8 TO
10 SERVINGS**

PREP TIME:
20 minutes

COOK TIME:
30 minutes

This isn't a complicated recipe, but no holiday would be complete without mashed potatoes. I like mine nice and creamy but with lots of lumps too. The key is in the texture, so you want to make sure you don't over mash these taters.

5 pounds Yukon Gold potatoes, peeled and quartered

Sea salt and freshly ground black pepper

1½ sticks (6 ounces) unsalted butter, sliced into 12 pieces, plus 3 tablespoons

½ teaspoon Tony Chachere's Creole Seasoning

¼ teaspoon garlic powder

¾ cup half-and-half

1. Add the potatoes to a large pot and fill with enough water to fully submerge. Season generously with salt and bring to a low boil over medium-high heat. Cook until fork tender, about 30 minutes. Drain the potatoes and return them to the pot.

2. Using a potato masher, gently mash the potatoes to release some of the steam, then add the butter pieces, Tony's seasoning, and garlic powder and mash some more. Once the butter has melted, add the half-and-half and stir well to combine. Season with salt and pepper.

3. Transfer the mashed potatoes to a large heatproof dish and dot with the remaining 3 tablespoons butter. Cover to keep warm until ready to serve.

Holiday Cheese Board

**MAKES 8 TO
10 SERVINGS**

PREP TIME:
20 minutes

We have a cheese board for just about every occasion because it's simple, beautiful, and a great appetizer to feed a big crowd. For a holiday like Thanksgiving or Christmas, I like to add seasonal fruits and flavors. Fall apples, pomegranate seeds, and festive accents like rosemary and cranberries add that special touch to your holiday spread.

8 ounces triple-cream brie cheese

8 ounces aged Parmesan cheese, thinly sliced

6 ounces Sartori BellaVitano Merlot cheese

3 ounces sliced cured sausage

3 ounces thinly sliced prosciutto

25 multigrain crackers

25 golden round crackers

2 cups cinnamon apple chips

2 Honeycrisp apples, cored and sliced

1 cup grapes

½ cup pomegranate seeds

½ cup Marcona almonds

Honey, for serving

Rosemary sprigs, for garnish (optional)

Arrange the cheeses, meats, crackers, apple chips, apple slices, grapes, pomegranate seeds, and almonds on a large platter or wooden serving board. Drizzle with honey and garnish with rosemary sprigs, if desired.

Pumpkin Cake

**MAKES
12 SERVINGS**

PREP TIME:
20 minutes

COOK TIME:
1 hour

When it's fall, everything is pumpkin! But even if you feel burned out on pumpkin recipes, this is one you can't pass over. This cake is so tender and moist from the canned pumpkin and olive oil, and it's spiced with a touch of cinnamon. I like to skip the traditional icing and just top it with a light dusting of powdered sugar, so you can soak in all that delicious pumpkin flavor.

Cooking spray, for the pan

2½ cups granulated sugar

1½ cups extra-virgin olive oil

3 large eggs

1 teaspoon pure vanilla extract

3 cups all-purpose flour

2 teaspoons ground cinnamon

2 teaspoons baking soda

½ teaspoon salt

1 (15-ounce) can unsweetened pumpkin puree

Powdered sugar, for serving

1. Preheat the oven to 350°F. Coat a 10-inch Bundt pan with cooking spray.

2. In the bowl of a stand mixer fitted with the paddle attachment or in a large bowl with a hand mixer, beat together the sugar and oil until thoroughly combined. Beat in the eggs one at a time, followed by the vanilla.

3. In a medium bowl, whisk together the flour, cinnamon, baking soda, and salt. Add the flour mixture and pumpkin puree to the egg mixture, one half at a time, and beat well.

4. Scoop the batter into the prepared Bundt pan. Bake until a toothpick inserted in the center of the cake comes out clean, about 1 hour.

5. Let the cake cool in the pan for 10 minutes before inverting onto a wire rack. Dust with powdered sugar and slice to serve.

12

Ooey, gooey, buttery, chocolaty, and all things in between—it's dessert time. Y'all know I love cookies of all kinds, but this time I want to share some of the other sweets that are near and dear to my heart. If I could make a book just about desserts I would, but for now enjoy these special treats that my family loves.

And Just Like That . . .

Time for Dessert

Sea Salt Double-Decadent Chocolate Chip Cookies

MAKES ABOUT 2 DOZEN COOKIES

PREP TIME:
10 minutes

COOK TIME:
10 minutes

I am the cookie queen, and everyone that knows me knows this. I can spot a good cookie just by eyeing it. I have a love affair with all kinds of cookies. They can put anyone in a good mood, and I don't trust anyone who doesn't like them. I could go on and on about my feelings for cookies, but let's just jump to this recipe that will change your life. Double chocolate chip cookies: double the chocolate, double the deliciousness, double Decker-dence (get it?).

You will feel conflicted every time you make cookies because you won't be able to choose between my OG classic chocolate chip cookies or these.

2 sticks (6 ounces) unsalted butter, softened

1 cup light brown sugar

¼ cup granulated sugar

2 teaspoons pure vanilla extract

1 large egg plus 1 large egg yolk

2 cups all-purpose flour

1 teaspoon baking soda

½ teaspoon sea salt

½ cup unsweetened cocoa powder

1½ cups semisweet chocolate chips

Flaky sea salt, for sprinkling

1. Preheat the oven to 350°F and line two baking sheets with silicone baking mats or parchment paper.

2. In a large bowl with a hand mixer or in the bowl of a stand mixer, cream the butter and both sugars until light and fluffy, about 3 minutes. Add the vanilla, whole egg, and egg yolk and continue to mix for another 2 minutes.

3. In a medium bowl, whisk together the flour, baking soda, salt, and cocoa powder. Add the dry ingredients to the wet ingredients and mix on low speed until combined, being careful not to overmix. Fold in the chocolate chips.

4. Portion the dough into 1½-tablespoon balls and arrange on the prepared baking sheets. Bake for 8 to 10 minutes or until the edges are set.

5. Remove the cookies from the oven and sprinkle with flaky sea salt. Transfer to a pretty platter and enjoy.

Southern Peach Cobbler

MAKES 8 SERVINGS

PREP TIME:
40 minutes

COOK TIME:
1 hour

CHILL TIME:
30 minutes

I remember my mama making this amazing peach cobbler when we were kids. She used an old recipe from *Southern Living* magazine, and it was just the best. I'll never forget that crust, so crisp and buttery. I think this cobbler is about as close as it gets.

FOR THE CRUST

2 2/3 cups all-purpose flour, plus more for rolling

1 teaspoon salt

1 cup cold all-vegetable shortening (I use Crisco)

2 to 3 tablespoons ice water

Cooking spray, for the baking dish

1 large egg, beaten with 1 teaspoon milk for the egg wash

FOR THE FILLING

2 pounds sliced peaches, fresh or frozen and thawed

1 1/4 cups plus 2 tablespoons sugar

3 tablespoons all-purpose flour

1 tablespoon fresh lemon juice

6 tablespoons unsalted butter

2 teaspoons pure vanilla extract

1 teaspoon ground cinnamon

1/4 teaspoon ground nutmeg

Vanilla ice cream, for serving

1. Make the crust: In a large bowl, whisk the flour and salt until combined. Using a pastry blender or fork, cut in the shortening until it's pea-size. Gradually add the ice water 1 tablespoon at a time, stirring continuously, until a soft dough comes together.

2. Shape the dough into a ball and divide in half. Flatten each half into a disk and wrap in plastic wrap. Chill for at least 30 minutes or up to 2 days.

3. Preheat the oven to 375°F and coat a 9 x 13-inch baking dish with cooking spray.

4. Make the filling: In a large bowl, combine the peaches, 1 1/4 cups sugar, the melted butter, flour, lemon juice, vanilla, cinnamon, and nutmeg and toss to coat. Set aside.

5. On a lightly floured work surface, roll out one disk of dough into a rectangle. Press into the prepared dish, then add the filling.

6. Roll out the second disk of dough into a large rectangle. Using a pizza cutter or sharp knife, slice the dough into 1-inch-thick strips. Place the strips of dough on top in a lattice formation.

7. Brush the top with the egg wash and sprinkle with 2 tablespoons sugar. Bake until the filling is bubbling and the crust is golden, about 1 hour. Serve warm with vanilla ice cream.

Deep-Dish Chocolate Chip Cookie Skillet

MAKES 10 TO 12 SERVINGS

PREP TIME: 10 minutes

COOK TIME: 30 minutes

What's better than a dozen chocolate chip cookies? A huge deep-dish skillet filled with melty chocolate chips and dusted with powdered sugar. Trust me when I say this will send even the most seasoned cookie lover over the top.

2 sticks (8 ounces) unsalted butter, softened

¾ cup granulated sugar

¾ cup packed brown sugar

2 large eggs

2 teaspoons pure vanilla extract

2 cups plus 2 tablespoons unbleached all-purpose flour

1 tablespoon cornstarch

1 teaspoon baking soda

1 teaspoon salt

1½ cups semisweet chocolate chips

¼ cup Nutella or melted chocolate, for filling

Powdered sugar, for dusting (optional)

1. Preheat the oven to 350°F.

2. In a large bowl with a hand mixer or in the bowl of a stand mixer, beat the butter and both sugars until light and fluffy, about 3 minutes. Add the eggs and vanilla and beat until fully combined.

3. In a separate bowl, whisk together the flour, cornstarch, baking soda, and salt. Add the dry ingredients to the wet ingredients and beat until combined. Fold in three-quarters of the chocolate chips.

4. Press half the cookie dough into a 10-inch cast-iron skillet. Spread with a layer of the Nutella, top with the remaining cookie dough, and sprinkle with the remaining chocolate chips.

5. Bake until the cookie is set and the edges are golden brown, 20 to 30 minutes (I like it a little underbaked so it's extra gooey). Top it off with a dusting of powdered sugar if you wanna go crazy!

Puppy Chow

**MAKES 10 TO
12 SERVINGS**

PREP TIME:
5 minutes

COOK TIME:
5 minutes

CHILL TIME:
20 minutes

The kids love making this! It's easy, fun, and very interactive. They'll eat this until it's gone, especially around the holidays. If you want to get festive, add colored M&M's that match the occasion: orange and brown for Halloween; green and red for Christmas; pink and purple for Easter; red, white, and blue for July Fourth. You get the drift!

10 cups Rice Chex
  cereal

8 tablespoons
  (1 stick) unsalted
  butter

1½ cups creamy
  peanut butter

2 cups semisweet
  chocolate chips

1 tablespoon pure
  vanilla extract

3½ cups powdered
  sugar

2 cups M&M's

1. Put the cereal in a large bowl and set aside.

2. In a small saucepan, bring about 2 inches of water to a boil over medium-high heat. In a heatproof bowl that will fit on top of the saucepan, combine the butter, peanut butter, and chocolate chips. Set the bowl on top of the saucepan. Reduce the heat to medium-low and cook, stirring constantly, until completely melted, 3 to 5 minutes. Remove from the heat and stir in the vanilla.

3. Pour the melted chocolate mixture over the cereal in the large bowl and stir to coat completely. Let cool for 5 minutes. Transfer to a large plastic bag and add the powdered sugar. Shake until evenly coated. Add the M&M's and shake again to mix. Line a baking sheet with parchment paper and pour out the cereal in an even layer. Chill in the refrigerator for 20 minutes to set before serving.

Brown Sugar Apple Pie

MAKES 6 TO 8 SERVINGS

PREP TIME:
25 minutes

COOK TIME:
1 hour

If you've never made an apple pie with brown sugar before, you're missing out! I love the deep and almost caramel-like flavor of the filling when you use only brown sugar. It's such a unique taste, and the mixture of the tart apples with the sweet, saucy filling and golden, crisp crust is amazing. Serve this pie at your holiday dinner and everyone will be begging for the recipe.

1 (2-count) package refrigerated piecrusts (I use Marie Callender's)

5 to 6 baking apples (such as Cortland, Empire, or Granny Smith), peeled, cored, and sliced

1 tablespoon fresh lemon juice

1/2 cup packed light brown sugar

1 tablespoon cornstarch

1 tablespoon all-purpose flour

1/2 teaspoon ground cinnamon

1/8 teaspoon salt

2 tablespoons unsalted butter, cut into small pats

1 large egg, beaten with 1 tablespoon milk for the egg wash

1. Position a rack in the center of the oven and preheat to 450°F. Wrap 1 piecrust in plastic wrap and put in the fridge. Use the other crust to line a 9-inch pie pan. Cover and chill in the fridge until the apple filling is ready.

2. In a large bowl, toss the apple slices with the lemon juice. Sprinkle with the brown sugar, cornstarch, flour, cinnamon, and salt and toss until coated. Pour the apple filling into the crust-lined pie pan and dot with the butter.

3. Place the second piecrust on top and press around the edges. Trim any excess, then crimp the edges to seal. Using a sharp knife, slice a few vents in the top crust for steam to escape. Brush with the egg wash.

4. Place the pie pan on a large rimmed baking sheet and bake for 10 minutes. Reduce the heat to 350°F and bake until well browned and bubbling, about 50 minutes. If the piecrust is browning too quickly, cover with foil. Let the pie cool completely, at least 1 hour, before slicing to serve.

Double-Trouble Chocolate Brownies

MAKES 9 BIG BROWNIES

PREP TIME:
15 minutes

COOK TIME:
40 minutes

Some people like cakier brownies and some like them soft and fudgy. Put me down for fudgy. I always make mine extra fudgy and loaded with big chocolate chunks, so you get that melty, gooey goodness in every bite! Here's how I make the most indulgent, decadent double-chocolate brownies.

2 sticks (8 ounces) unsalted butter, melted and cooled

1 cup light brown sugar

1 cup granulated sugar

¼ teaspoon salt

3 large eggs

2 teaspoons pure vanilla extract

¾ cup all-purpose flour

4 ounces unsweetened cocoa powder

1 (8-ounce) bar dark chocolate, roughly chopped

Powdered sugar, for dusting (optional)

1. Preheat the oven to 350°F and line an 8-inch square pan with parchment paper.

2. In a large bowl, combine the butter, both sugars, and salt. Mix until smooth, then whisk in the eggs and vanilla until frothy and pale.

3. In a separate bowl, combine the flour and cocoa powder and mix well. Add the flour mixture to the egg mixture and stir until all the flour is incorporated. Fold in three-quarters of the chopped chocolate.

4. Scoop the batter into the prepared pan and top with the rest of the chocolate. Bake until the center is mostly set but still soft, 35 to 40 minutes. The brownies will firm up as they cool, so be careful not to overbake!

5. Remove from the oven and let cool in the pan for at least 30 minutes. If you really want to add that extra kick of sugar, sift some powdered sugar on top.

Caramel Cake

MAKES 8 TO 12 SERVINGS

PREP TIME:
40 minutes

COOK TIME:
50 minutes

There is something extra Southern and comforting about a caramel cake. Just like pecan pie or peach cobbler, this is a staple in the South. One of the best slices of caramel cake I've ever had was in Georgia, at a girlfriend's house when I was in middle school. Her mama had just made the cake, and it wasn't quite ready to be cut, but my friend insisted we sneak a taste. I just remember it melting in my mouth; I never forgot all the delicious brown sugar flavors. Here is my version.

FOR THE CAKE

- 3 cups all-purpose flour
- 1½ tablespoons baking powder
- 1 teaspoon salt
- 2 sticks (8 ounces) unsalted butter, softened and cubed
- 2 cups granulated sugar
- 4 large eggs
- 1½ tablespoons pure vanilla extract
- 1 cup buttermilk

FOR THE FROSTING

- 1½ cups light brown sugar
- 1½ cups dark brown sugar
- 2½ sticks (10 ounces) unsalted butter, softened and cubed
- ½ cup buttermilk
- ½ cup heavy cream
- 1 tablespoon pure vanilla extract
- 1 teaspoon almond extract
- Pinch of salt

1. Preheat the oven to 350°F and line two round cake pans with parchment paper. (Do not grease the pans—the cake won't rise properly if you do.)

2. Make the cake: In a medium bowl, whisk together the flour, baking powder, and salt.

3. In a large bowl with a hand mixer or in the bowl of a stand mixer, beat the butter until creamy, about 2 minutes. Add the granulated sugar and continue to beat, until light and fluffy. With the mixer running, add the eggs one at a time until incorporated, followed by the vanilla.

4. Slowly add the flour mixture and buttermilk in alternating additions and beat until fully incorporated. Immediately divide the batter between the prepared pans, spreading it evenly in each pan.

5. Bake until the tops are lightly golden and a toothpick poked into the center comes out clean, about 30 minutes. Remove the cakes from the oven and let cool in the pans for 15 minutes.

You can make the frosting ahead of time and keep it chilled. Let it come to room temperature before using. Warm frosting will pour and ooze over the cake; room temperature frosting will be thicker and more spreadable.

6. Make the frosting (see note): In a large saucepan, over medium heat, combine the light and dark brown sugars, the butter, buttermilk, heavy cream, vanilla, almond extract, and salt and bring to a soft boil, stirring, until the sugar is completely dissolved, 6 to 8 minutes.

7. Once the mixture starts to bubble around the edges, reduce the heat to low and continue to cook for 10 minutes, stirring regularly. If you have a candy thermometer, the caramel should not reach more than 220°F.

8. Remove from the heat to cool for 3 minutes, then transfer to the bowl of a stand mixer and beat until it begins to lose its glossiness and has a spreadable consistency, about 5 minutes. (Or, transfer to a large bowl and beat with a whisk for about 10 minutes.)

9. Assemble the cake: Place one of the cakes on a plate or cake stand and spread a quarter of the frosting in an even layer. Add the top cake layer and half of the remaining frosting on top, smoothing as you go. This should be a thin layer of frosting. Use the remaining frosting to cover the whole cake until coated. If the frosting begins to seize, just dip your knife in hot water and slowly work.

Bananas Foster

MAKES 2 SERVINGS

PREP TIME:
5 minutes

COOK TIME:
5 minutes

One night, after a lovely dinner, Eric was wondering what we had for dessert. We were low on groceries because we were about to leave to go out of town, so I looked around. I had everything to make bananas foster, but I had never made it before. I gave it a go, and everyone loved it!

3 tablespoons salted butter

3 tablespoons packed brown sugar

1 teaspoon ground cinnamon, plus more for serving

1 banana, sliced

2 tablespoons rum

Vanilla ice cream, for serving

1. In an 8- or 10-inch cast-iron skillet, melt the butter over medium-low heat. Add the brown sugar and cinnamon and cook, stirring, until the sugar melts, about 30 seconds. Add the banana and cook, stirring frequently, until softened, about 1 minute.

2. Add the rum and cook until the sauce begins to simmer, about 3 minutes. Tip the pan away from you and light the rum with a long lighter. Keep a fire extinguisher and the lid handy just in case! Let the fire go out.

3. Scoop ice cream into two bowls and spoon the caramelized bananas on top. Dust with cinnamon and enjoy!

13

Let's shake things up, because it's cocktail time, baby! These are some fun cocktails that will become party favorites for sure. I've put together a good variety of drinks throughout this book (check out the Italy & Greece chapter next), but these drinks are my anytime favorites. I especially love the espresso martini because it just instantly makes you smile!

Who says you have to open a bottle of wine to unwind? Why not mix things up after a long day and shake, shake, shake it up with a sexy little cocktail and a bubble bath? Enjoy!

Drinks

Hunch Punch

MAKES 10 TO 15 SERVINGS

PREP TIME:
5 minutes

If you've never had hunch punch, it's basically a big punch bowl full of everything that tastes good, plus booze. Be careful, though, because it doesn't taste like there's alcohol in it and can sneak up on you quick!

These measurements are meant for a small gathering, but you can easily double or triple the recipe for a larger group. Be sure to refrigerate all the ingredients for at least 2 hours before making the punch.

Ice

8 ounces orange juice

8 ounces pineapple juice

8 ounces lemonade, regular or light

8 ounces ginger ale (I like Zevia)

8 ounces lemon-lime soda (I like Zevia)

8 ounces vodka

4 ounces coconut rum (I use Malibu)

3 oranges, sliced, plus more slices for serving

8 ounces maraschino cherries, drained, plus more for serving

1. Fill a large punch bowl with ice. Add the orange and pineapple juices, lemonade, ginger ale, lemon-lime soda, vodka, and rum. Stir in the orange slices and cherries.

2. Ladle the punch into cups and serve garnished with more orange slices and cherries.

Espresso Martini

MAKES 1 DRINK

PREP TIME:
5 minutes

This is one of my favorite drinks to order when I'm out with the girls. I love everything about it: how it looks, tastes, and smells. One of my best girlfriends, Lora, makes the best espresso martini you will ever have and it's the reason I fell in love with this drink. It's the perfect boozy coffee cocktail for a girls' night out or, better yet, a girls' night in!

1.5 ounces vodka

1.5 ounces strong espresso, cooled

1 ounce coffee liqueur

1 ounce Irish Cream liqueur (I use Bailey's)

Ice

3 whole coffee beans

Cocoa powder, for dusting (optional)

1. In a cocktail shaker, combine the vodka, espresso, coffee liqueur, and Irish cream and shake well. Add ice and shake vigorously.

2. Strain into a martini glass and garnish with the coffee beans. Dust with a little cocoa powder if desired.

Grapefruit Paloma

MAKES 1 DRINK

PREP TIME:
5 minutes

I could never get sick of a margarita, but when I want something a little different, a paloma is my next choice! It's still got the light, citrusy flavors of a margarita but with a bite of grapefruit and a splash of sparkling water. Have one or two poolside with some mango ceviche or shrimp tacos!

2 ounces fresh grapefruit juice, plus 2 grapefruit wedges

Kosher salt

.5 ounces fresh lime juice

1 to 2 teaspoons agave

2 ounces Tequila

Ice

2 ounces sparkling water

1. Run 1 grapefruit wedge around the rim of a highball glass and dip the rim in salt.

2. In the glass, combine the grapefruit juice, lime juice, and agave. Stir in the tequila, add ice, and top off with the sparkling water. Garnish with the remaining grapefruit wedge.

Coconut Lemonade

MAKES 1 DRINK

PREP TIME:
5 minutes

This coconut lemonade is a refreshing drink that tastes like a tropical vacation! You can make it with or without alcohol, but I love it with a good pour of Malibu coconut rum.

8 fresh mint leaves, plus a sprig of mint for garnish

¼ teaspoon stevia or sugar

2 lemon slices, plus 2 tablespoons fresh lemon juice

2 lime slices (plus 1 more for garnish), plus 2 tablespoons fresh lime juice

Ice

8 ounces coconut water

4 ounces canned unsweetened coconut milk, shaken

4 ounces coconut rum (optional)

1. In the bottom of a large glass, muddle the mint leaves, stevia, and lemon and lime slices with a muddler or pestle.

2. Put some ice in a blender. Add the coconut water, coconut milk, lemon juice, lime juice, and your desired amount of rum (if using). Blend until smooth.

3. Pour the coconut mixture into the glass with the muddled mint mixture. Garnish with the mint sprig and lime slice.

14

In May and June 2021 my family and I took an incredible twenty-six-day trip to Greece and Italy. While we were there, I made it a point to find places I could work alongside some of the most incredible cooks. I learned so much about food and how to use ingredients in ways I had never thought of.

I'm so excited to share some of the special dishes I experienced in Greece and Italy, and I hope you love them too.

Italy & Greece
2021

Recipes with ○ icon indicate "Good for Ya!" recipes.

Aperol Spritz

MAKES 1 DRINK

PREP TIME:
5 minutes

Eric and I had the pleasure of taking an incredibly dreamy trip off the coast of Italy and France with a good friend of ours. When we arrived on the big fancy boat, we were handed the most delicious, refreshing, and needed cocktail after a long day of travel. Italians just do it right with this one, among many other things!

Ice

3 ounces (6 tablespoons) prosecco, chilled

2 ounces (¼ cup) Aperol, chilled

1 ounce (2 tablespoons) soda water

1 orange wedge, for garnish (see note)

1. Grab a large wine glass and fill it with ice.

2. Add the prosecco first, followed by the Aperol, followed by the soda water.

3. Stir gently, then garnish with the orange wedge.

Jessie's note:

I like to use blood orange when it's in season and add an extra flare with a sprig of rosemary (if you wanna get real crazy).

Limoncello

**MAKES ABOUT
7 CUPS**

PREP TIME:
4 days to 1 month

COOK TIME:
10 minutes

CHILL TIME:
4 hours

In Italy, limoncello is served as a digestif to finish off a meal. It's light and bright with just the right amount of alcohol for sipping. First, you infuse liquor with the freshest lemons you can find, then you mix the infused spirit with simple syrup and let it rest for weeks to build flavor. It's a labor of love that takes time, but the end result is worth the effort!

8 large unwaxed organic lemons, washed and dried

4 cups pure vodka (preferably 100-proof, but you can also use 80-proof)

3 cups filtered water

3 cups sugar

1. Using a sharp knife or a vegetable peeler, peel the lemons. You want only the yellow part (the white is the bitter part, so try to get as little of it on the peel as possible). Put the lemon peels in a 1-quart jar and cover with the vodka. Seal and let infuse somewhere out of direct sunlight for at least 4 days or up to 1 month. The longer you let it sit, the lemonier your limoncello will be!

2. To strain, line a funnel with cheesecloth (or use a fine-mesh strainer) and set it over a large bowl or pitcher. Strain the vodka into the bowl, stirring it in the strainer if the flow stops.

3. In a saucepan, combine the filtered water and sugar and bring to a boil over medium-high heat, stirring occasionally, until the sugar is completely dissolved, 5 to 7 minutes. Remove from the heat and let cool to room temperature.

4. Pour the cooled syrup into the infused vodka 1 cup at a time until it reaches your desired sweetness. Portion the limoncello into bottles and chill in the fridge for at least 4 hours before drinking. Limoncello will keep in the fridge for up to a month or in the freezer for up to a year.

Marinated Olives

MAKES 6 TO 8 SERVINGS

PREP TIME:
10 minutes

CHILL TIME:
4 hours

2 cups pitted green olives

2 cups pitted Kalamata olives

3 or 4 cloves garlic, thinly sliced

2 teaspoons lemon zest

2 tablespoons fresh lemon juice

½ teaspoon crushed red pepper flakes (optional, if you like it spicy)

1 teaspoon Italian seasoning

¼ cup extra-virgin olive oil

Flaky sea salt

I put these in a little bowl alongside my cheese and other grazing snacks while people arrive or while I'm cooking. I loved eating olives and cheese so much when we were in Greece, and they are my go-to snack these days.

Layer the olives in a mason jar with the garlic, lemon zest, lemon juice, pepper flakes (if using), and Italian seasoning. Pour in the oil and seal the jar. Refrigerate for at least 1 hour before serving. The marinated olives will keep in the fridge for up to 2 weeks.

Good for Ya!

Italy-Inspired Cheese Board

MAKES 8 SERVINGS

PREP TIME:
15 minutes

1 (4-ounce) block Parmesan cheese

1 (8-ounce) wheel triple-cream brie cheese

4 ounces Manchego cheese

4 ounces Genoa salami

4 ounces prosciutto

1 to 2 cups Marinated Olives (above)

2 to 3 peaches, sliced

2 to 3 bunches green or red grapes

1 cup Marcona almonds

Assorted crackers and sliced French baguette

1 (8.5-ounce) jar fig jam

1 (6-ounce) jar wildflower honey

In Italy it's common to serve an aperitivo with your appetizer, and this is the perfect board with which to do so. An aperitivo is a pre-meal drink meant to open the stomach and get you ready for a nice meal. Serve this beautiful appetizer with a nice Aperol Spritz (page 255) to really get in the mood!

On a large tray or wooden serving board, arrange the cheeses and meats, followed by the olives, peaches, grapes, almonds, and crackers. Put the jam and honey in separate small serving bowls and place on the tray.

Greek Feta Salad

MAKES 6 SERVINGS

PREP TIME:
15 minutes

This salad is one of my favorite things we ate on our trip. It's light, fresh, and bursting with flavor from the basil and salty feta. I love the simplicity of this recipe—it takes only a handful of ingredients to make the most amazing salad that's both healthy and filling.

1 pint cherry tomatoes, halved, or 4 Roma tomatoes, cut into bite-size pieces

1 English cucumber, peeled and sliced ½ inch thick

½ small red onion, sliced

½ green bell pepper, sliced into strips

6 ounces good feta cheese, cut into ¼-inch cubes

¼ cup extra-virgin olive oil

3 tablespoons white wine vinegar

2 tablespoons chopped fresh basil

3 tablespoons chopped fresh parsley

1 teaspoon sea salt, plus more as needed

½ teaspoon freshly ground black pepper

1 teaspoon Italian seasoning

In a large bowl, toss the tomatoes, cucumber, onion, bell pepper, and feta. Add the oil, vinegar, basil, parsley, salt, and pepper. Toss gently until everything is combined. Sprinkle with the Italian seasoning. Taste and add more salt if needed. Serve cold.

Good for Ya!

Tzatziki

MAKES 5 TO
6 SERVINGS

PREP TIME:
15 minutes

Tzatziki is a Greek essential that's made of thick, creamy yogurt, garlic, and grated cucumber. It's a great topping for meats or veggies, or it can be served as a dip with soft, warm pita bread. This is an authentic recipe that we had on our trip and, let me tell you, it's so much better than any store-bought tzatziki you can get! My one tip is to season it and keep tasting as you go to achieve the right balance of tangy and salty.

1 large English cucumber, halved lengthwise and seeds removed

Sea salt and freshly ground black pepper

1 (16-ounce) container plain Greek yogurt

4 cloves garlic, finely grated

¼ cup extra-virgin olive oil, plus more for drizzling

1 tablespoon white vinegar

Warm pita bread, for serving

1. Grate the cucumber into a large bowl and sprinkle with salt. Transfer to a fine-mesh strainer or some cheesecloth and gently squeeze out the extra liquid. Return to the bowl and stir in the Greek yogurt.

2. Add the garlic, oil, and vinegar and whisk everything together until creamy. Season with salt and pepper and drizzle with more olive oil. Serve with warm pita bread for dipping. This is also great as a topping for chicken or beef.

Moussaka

MAKES 6 TO
8 SERVINGS

PREP TIME:
1 hour

COOK TIME:
2 hours 30 minutes

If you've never had moussaka, think of it like a lasagna, but instead of noodles you layer fried or baked eggplant and potato rounds. Then you have a deliciously meaty sauce in between the layers, and a creamy white sauce on top to seal in all the flavor.

FOR THE VEGETABLES

- 4 eggplants, sliced into ¼-inch-thick rounds
- Sea salt
- 2 tablespoons extra-virgin olive oil, plus more for greasing
- 4 large russet or Yukon Gold potatoes, peeled and halved
- Extra-virgin olive oil or cooking spray, for the baking dish
- ½ cup grated Parmesan cheese

FOR THE MEAT SAUCE

- 2 tablespoons extra-virgin olive oil
- 2 yellow onions, finely chopped
- ½ pound ground beef
- 3 tomatoes, diced
- 1 clove garlic, minced
- ½ teaspoon sugar
- 1 bay leaf
- ¼ teaspoon ground cumin
- ¼ teaspoon dried oregano
- Sea salt and freshly ground black pepper

FOR THE BÉCHAMEL SAUCE

- 6 tablespoons unsalted butter
- 1 cup all-purpose flour
- 2 cups whole milk, warmed, plus more as needed
- ½ cup grated Parmesan cheese
- ⅛ teaspoon ground nutmeg
- Sea salt and freshly ground black pepper

1. Preheat the oven to 400°F and line two baking sheets with parchment paper.

2. Make the vegetables: Sprinkle the eggplant generously with salt to cut the bitterness and let rest for about 30 minutes. Rinse and pat dry. Arrange the slices on the prepared baking sheets and drizzle with the oil. Roast until lightly browned and softened, about 20 minutes. Remove from the oven and set aside. Keep the oven on.

3. Place the potatoes in a large pot and fill with enough water to cover completely. Bring to a boil over medium-high heat. Cook until tender, about 15 minutes. Drain and transfer to a cutting board. When cool enough to handle, thinly slice the potatoes and set aside.

4. Make the meat sauce: In a large skillet, heat the oil over medium heat. Add the onions and cook until softened and slightly caramelized, 7 to 8 minutes. Add the ground beef and cook, breaking up the meat with a wooden spoon, until browned, about 8 minutes.

5. Add the tomatoes, garlic, sugar, bay leaf, cumin, oregano, and salt and pepper. Mix well and let the sauce come to a simmer, then cover, reduce the heat to medium-low, and cook until thickened, about 30 minutes.

6. Make the béchamel sauce: In another large skillet, melt the butter over low heat. Slowly add the flour, whisking continuously, until beginning to thicken, about 5 minutes. Add the milk in a steady stream, whisking continuously, until the mixture is nice and smooth, about 1 minute. Stir in the Parmesan, then season with the nutmeg and salt and pepper. Mix well and add a little more milk if the sauce seems too thick.

7. To assemble the moussaka: Coat a 9 x 13-inch baking dish with oil or cooking spray. Evenly layer the potato slices in the dish, followed by the eggplant slices. Top with an even layer of the meat sauce. (You can do another layer of potatoes and eggplant if you have extra.) Top evenly with the béchamel, then sprinkle evenly with the Parmesan.

8. Bake the moussaka, uncovered, until lightly golden brown on top, about 30 minutes. Remove from the oven and let cool for about 10 minutes before slicing to serve.

Fresh Pasta

**MAKES 4 TO
6 SERVINGS**

PREP TIME:
1 hour

COOK TIME:
5 minutes

One year Eric bought me a pasta maker, and I was so excited. I made fresh pasta that day with my Bolognese sauce to go with it, and I was in love. The whole process of pasta making is very soothing, and the result is like nothing else. When we were in Italy, I had the chance to learn to make fresh pasta again, and it reignited my love for it. Here's my basic recipe for making spaghetti or fettuccine. Serve it with Bolognese or my classic Meat Sauce (page 269).

2 cups all-purpose flour, plus more as needed

3 large eggs

½ tablespoon extra-virgin olive oil

½ teaspoon sea salt

1. Place the flour in a mound on a clean work surface. Make a well in the center and add the eggs, oil, and salt. Mix with your fingers or a fork, gradually pulling in the flour from the bottom and sides of the well. This process should go slow. It will look like a slurry before it comes together into a soft dough. (It's OK if you don't use every bit of flour!)

2. Knead the dough until soft and pliable, 8 to 10 minutes, At the beginning, it may feel dry, but just keep working it. If it still seems very dry and tough after a few minutes, wet your fingers with a little water and work it into the dough. Shape the dough into a ball, cover in plastic wrap, and let rest at room temperature for 30 minutes. Dust 2 large baking sheets with flour and set aside.

3. Slice the dough into 4 pieces. Flatten 1 piece of dough into an oval disk. Run it through your pasta maker's roller attachment three times on level 1. It will be in a long oval shape. Next lay it out flat and find the center of the dough piece. Fold both the left and right ends into that center line, then fold it in half.

4. Run the dough through the roller attachment three times on level 2, three times on level 3, and one time each on levels 4, 5, and 6. Now you'll have a very long strip of dough. Depending on how long you want your noodles, cut the strip of dough into 2 or 3 sections. Transfer to one of the prepared baking sheets.

5. Repeat steps 3 and 4 with the remaining 3 pieces of dough until you have a total of about 12 thin dough sheets. Sprinkle them all with flour so they don't stick together or to the machine.

6. Working in batches, run the pasta sheets through your pasta maker's cutter attachment to make your desired shape—spaghetti or fettuccine. Toss each batch with flour and mound on the baking sheets while you cut the others.

7. In a large pot of salted boiling water, cook the pasta until al dente, 4 to 5 minutes. If not ready to cook right away, lay the noodles on a pasta rack to dry until brittle, then store in an airtight container for up to 2 weeks.

Meat Sauce

MAKES 4 SERVINGS

PREP TIME:
15 minutes

COOK TIME:
3 hours 20 minutes

This sauce is very thick and slow-cooked to perfection, just like they do it in Italy. It has no butter and no heavy cream, but the flavor turns out so rich.

2 tablespoons extra-virgin olive oil

¼ cup diced onion

¼ cup chopped celery

¼ cup diced carrots

½ pound ground beef

½ pound ground pork

½ pound ground veal

¼ cup red wine

2 cups tomato sauce

Sea salt and freshly ground black pepper

¼ cup vegetable broth

Fresh Pasta (page 266), for serving

1. In a large skillet, heat the oil over medium-low heat. Add the onion, celery, and carrots and cook until softened, 7 to 10 minutes. Add the ground meats, increase the heat to medium, and cook, breaking up the meat with a wooden spoon, until browned, about 8 minutes.

2. Add the wine and increase the heat to medium-high. Once some of the alcohol cooks off, about 30 seconds, add the tomato sauce and season with salt and pepper. Mix well, then add the vegetable broth. Reduce the heat to medium-low and let simmer for 3 hours. Serve with fresh pasta.

Tomato Fritters

MAKES 6 SERVINGS

PREP TIME:
40 minutes

COOK TIME:
10 minutes

Santorini is known for their amazing tomatoes, and this recipe for tomato fritters is a specialty. Eric and I had the opportunity to make these on our trip alongside a chef who taught us all the little tricks for getting the perfect fritters. They are crisp and bursting with sweet tomatoes and herby goodness. I highly recommend serving these with my fresh Tzatziki (page 263)!

2 pints ripe cherry tomatoes, halved, plus more if needed

1 small red onion, finely chopped

2 tablespoons finely chopped fresh mint

2 tablespoons finely chopped fresh parsley

Sea salt and freshly ground black pepper

1 cup all-purpose flour

Extra-virgin olive oil, for frying

1. Add the cherry tomatoes to a medium bowl along with the onion, mint, and parsley. Season with salt and pepper. Using your hands or the back of a wooden spoon, mash the mixture together. Slowly add the flour until it begins to hold together and has the consistency of a thick batter. You can add more tomatoes if your batter is too dry, but avoid adding extra flour because it will dull the seasoning and flavor. Refrigerate for 30 minutes.

2. Fill a deep 12-inch skillet with enough oil to shallow fry, about 1 inch, and heat over high heat until very hot, 1 to 2 minutes. Working in batches of two to three, scoop spoonfuls of the batter into the hot oil. Fry until deeply golden, about 2 minutes per side. Transfer to a paper towel–lined plate to drain. Serve hot.

Tiramisu

MAKES 8 SERVINGS

PREP TIME:
20 minutes

CHILL TIME:
3 hours

I have never cared much for tiramisu, but when we had it freshly prepared in Italy, I fell in love. It didn't taste anything like the tiramisu I'd had before, so I knew I had to include this authentic recipe in my book!

2 pasteurized large egg yolks

½ cup sugar

1 cup heavy cream

1 (9-ounce) container mascarpone cheese

1 cup espresso

About 20 ladyfingers (use more or fewer depending on the size of your pan)

Unsweetened cocoa powder, for dusting

1. In a large bowl, beat the egg yolks and sugar until smooth and pale yellow, 3 to 5 minutes. In a separate bowl, whip the heavy cream to stiff peaks, 4 to 5 minutes.

2. Stir the mascarpone cheese in its container to remove any lumps, then add to the egg yolk mixture and mix well. Gently fold in the whipped cream.

3. Pour the espresso into a shallow dish and dip the ladyfingers in the coffee for about 2 seconds. Place half the ladyfingers in a serving dish in an even layer. Spread with half the cream mixture, then layer the remaining ladyfingers evenly on top. Spread with the remaining cream mixture and refrigerate for 3 hours to set. Dust generously with cocoa powder and slice to serve.

Focaccia

MAKES 4 TO
6 SERVINGS

PREP TIME:
2 hours

COOK TIME:
30 minutes

Every time I go to one of my favorite tapas restaurants in town, I order the focaccia bread to start. I'm drooling just thinking about the yummy, warm, flaky bread that melts in my mouth as the olive oil and sea salt coat my lips. If you want to make this girl happy, bring me a basket of bread and olive oil. You'll have me forever—ha! This recipe takes some time, but it's so addictive. It's the perfect predinner starter with a glass of wine.

4 cups all-purpose flour

2½ teaspoons salt

1 (¼ ounce) packet instant yeast (2¼ teaspoons)

1¾ cups lukewarm water

5 tablespoons extra-virgin olive oil

1 tablespoon dried rosemary

Flaky sea salt

Destin Dipping Oil (page 38), for serving

1. In a large bowl, whisk together the flour, salt, and instant yeast. Add the water. Using a rubber spatula, mix until the liquid is absorbed and a sticky dough begins to form. Rub the dough and the sides of the bowl with 1 tablespoon of oil. Cover the bowl with plastic wrap and place in a warm, draft-free part of the kitchen to rise for 30 minutes.

2. After the first rise, oil your hands and deflate the dough by pulling it away from the sides of the bowl and toward the center in a folding motion. Rotate the bowl a quarter turn as you keep pulling the dough up and away from the edge of the bowl and folding it in on itself. Repeat two more times for a total of four folds. Cover the bowl with plastic wrap and let rise for 1 hour, repeating the four-fold pattern again at the 30-minute mark.

3. Once the dough has finished its final rise, preheat the oven to 425°F and grease a 9 x 13-inch baking sheet with 2 tablespoons oil.

4. Turn the dough out onto the prepared sheet and very gently pull to the edges of the sheet. (If the dough is too firm, let rest for 5 minutes first.) Cover with plastic wrap and let rest for 30 minutes.

5. Sprinkle the dough with the rosemary, then drizzle with the remaining 2 tablespoons oil. Rub your hands lightly in the oil to coat, then, using all your fingers, press straight down to create deep dimples in the dough. Sprinkle all over with flaky sea salt.

6. Transfer to the oven and bake until golden and crisp, 25 to 30 minutes. Transfer the focaccia to a rack to cool for 10 minutes before slicing and serving with my Destin dipping oil—it's the perfect combo!

Acknowledgments

I want to thank my amazing team at HarperCollins for believing in me and supporting my dream to write my second cookbook! Lisa Sharkey, for always being my cheerleader and helping me make my cookbook dreams happen. Matt Harper, for his patience and for staying on top of me to get the book finished on time (LOL). Also at HarperCollins, a huge thank-you to Anna Montague, Maddie Pillari, Rachel Meyers, Jennifer Chung, Julie Paulauski, and Kendra Newton.

I also want to thank my amazing agents, Sloane and Margaret, at William Morris Endeavor for being my badass squad and supporting me through the entire process.

Thank you to my amazing team of photographers, John Hillin, who helped photograph this oh-so-delicious cookbook, and Liz Schoch, who brought my food to life through her beautiful food photos and styling. To Alex White from Milk and Honey Food Company for the beautiful food styling and tireless chopping, arranging, and reheating for the perfect ooey-gooey cheese pull.

To my fabulous Kittenish team, Rebecca O'Connor and Sarah Robinson, for making sure I look fashionably fabulous and to Tatum Hall for your creative eye and just "getting my homey vibe." To Taylor Eschbach for being my Ruby and helping me in everything I do! And to my glam squad, Jessica Payne and Carly Bethel, for making your girl feel pretty for the cookbook shoot. It truly takes a whole squad to bring my vision to life, and I couldn't do this without you!!

Index

Note: Page references in *italics* indicate photographs.

E

Edamame
Shrimp Fried Rice, 172, *173*
Eggplant
Fried, *50*, 51
Moussaka, 264–65, *265*
Egg(s)
Deviled, *36*, 37
Grilled Chicken Cobb Salad, 66, *67*
Karen's Quiche, *18*, 19
Mini Frittata, Muffins, *14*, 15
Sausage Biscuit Casserole, *10*, 11
Shrimp Fried Rice, 172, *173*
Tuna Sangwiches, *162*, 163
Espresso
Martini, *246*, 247
Tiramisu, *272*, 273

F

Fairy Cakes, *190*, 191
Fish
Pan-Seared Grouper with Tomato Jam, *166*, 167
Smoked Tuna Dip, 48, *49*
Tacos, Baja Babe, 164, *165*
Tuna Sangwiches, *162*, 163
Focaccia, 274–75, *275*
French Kiss Toast, 12, *13*
Frittata Egg Muffins, Mini, *14*, 15
Fritters, Tomato, 270, *271*
Fruit. *See also* Berries; *specific fruits*
Hunch Punch, 244, *245*

G

Garlic
Cheddar Biscuits, 52, *53*
Tzatziki, *262*, 263
Garlic powder, xi
Ginger-Lemon Immunity Shots, *2*, 3
"Good for Ya!" stickers, xi
Granola Bars, *186*, 187
Grapefruit Paloma, 247
Grapes
Holiday Cheese Board, 217, *218–19*
Italy-Inspired Cheese Board, 259
Greek Feta Salad, 260, *261*
Green beans
Chicken Thigh Bake, 86, *87*
Turkey Potpie, 156, *157*

Greens. *See also specific greens*
Christmas Wreath Salad, 210, *211*
Peach and Goat Cheese Salad, 62, *63*
Grouper, Pan-Seared, with Tomato Jam, *166*, 167

H

Ham. *See also* Prosciutto
Karen's Quiche, *18*, 19
Monte Cristo, *22*, 23
Haystacks, Butterscotch, 202, *203*
Honey
Brussels Sprouts, Oven-Roasted, 112, *113*
Classic Cheese Board, 38, *40–41*
Holiday Cheese Board, 217, *218–19*
Hot Dogs and Mash, Yaya's, 178, *179*
Hunch Punch, 244, *245*
Hush Puppies, *118*, 119

I

Immunity Shots, Lemon-Ginger, *2*, 3
Italy-Inspired Cheese Board, 259

J

Jam, Tomato, *166*, 167

L

Ladyfingers
Tiramisu, *272*, 273
Lamb, Roasted Rack of, *208*, 209
Lasagna, Ground Beef, 104, *105*
Latte, Pumpkin Spice, *200*, 201
Lemonade, Coconut, 248, *249*
Lemon(s)
Coconut Lemonade, 248, *249*
-Ginger Immunity Shots, *2*, 3
Limoncello, 256, *257*
Lentil Soup for the Soul, 70, *71*
Lettuce
Caesar Salad by Yours Truly, 58, *59*
Go-To Mexican Chopped Salad, *64*, 65
Grilled Chicken Cobb Salad, 66, *67*
Limoncello, 256, *257*
Lobster Risotto, 160, *161*
Louisiana Beignets, 16, *17*

About the Author

Singer-songwriter, TV personality, fashion designer, beauty and lifestyle influencer/entrepreneur, and two-time *New York Times* bestselling author Jessie James Decker has emerged as a multiplatform juggernaut, juggling fashion brands like her hugely successful fashion brand Kittenish—with three retail stores and growing—along with her television-hosting duties. Jessie's passion for music has made the multitalented Warner Music Nashville artist one of music's true breakout firebrands. On her 2009 self-titled debut, the singer's authentic style immediately captivated listeners everywhere. She continued to keep it real with her second studio album, 2017's *Southern Girl City Lights*, which debuted at No. 1 on Billboard's Top Country Albums chart. Now it's onto a new musical chapter of growth and empowerment with *The Woman I've Become* EP. Jessie was a fan favorite on the most recent season of *Dancing with Stars*, proving she really can do it all. Jessie lives with her husband, retired NFL player Eric Decker, and their three children, in Nashville, Tennessee.

HarperCollins books may be purchased for educational, business, or sales promotional use. For information, please email the Special Markets Department at SPsales@harpercollins.com.

FIRST EDITION

Designed by Jennifer Chung
Food photography by Liz Schoch
Lifestyle photography by John Hillin

Library of Congress Cataloging-in-Publication Data has been applied for.

ISBN 978-0-06-321060-8

23 24 25 26 27 TC 10 9 8 7 6 5 4 3 2 1